What I especially love about Chris[   ]that they are doubly-grounded. They are g[   ]particular passion for making Bible truth thoroughly, cheeriuii, _[   ]stood and loved, whether his intended audience is adult or child. But these hymns are also grounded in contemporary British, generally urban, life; they have a context, even the ones that are not specifically commissioned, reminding believers that living for Christ is in the now, in the time and place God's providence has placed us.

Ann Benton, author and housewife, Surrey

Back in 1972, when we were finalising *Psalm Praise*, my eye and ear were often pleasantly struck by the name of Christopher Idle—writing lyrics in widely contrasting styles, including one that remains a secure favourite in my own heart, Revelation 21–22 beautifully condensed in 'Then I saw a new heaven and earth'. The expectation raised here is repeated in some great songs written to well-known national tunes: 'Christ is surely coming' with Elgar's Pomp and Circumstance March No.1; and performances that I've conducted in a heaving Royal Albert Hall. Words to the Trumpet Voluntary, 'Men of Harlech' or 'Marching through Georgia' all had their 'Prom Praise' treatment. For Chris and his pen, mind and heart I'm for ever thankful.

Prof Noël Tredinnick, composer, teacher, music director; London

In the southern part of Africa, Chris Idle would be called a 'Madala'—someone who has grown older, who has experienced more and therefore is wiser to see beyond the here and the now. He stays in contact with loved ones and others who went before him. The texts of Chris Idle reveal his deep faith and expectation; they speak of prophets and pilgrims, of saints and of angels; of darkness and disappointments and light; of trees and beetles and everyday people. They connect us with the community in heaven and on earth. They urge us to change the present—and they give us a glimpse of what is to come.

Prof Elsabé Kloppers, University of South Africa

Christopher Idle always delights with his hymns—they are so biblical in their statements and allusion and so theological in their thoughts and intentions. Like the man himself, the hymns are soaked in the gospel message of our Creator's great work of redemption.

Phillip Jensen, Two Ways Ministries, Sydney, NSW

As a church pastor hunting for material to sing during the Sunday service, I keep finding myself locating one of Chris's hymns which fits the bill. Why is this? The hymns are biblical, in faithfulness to the text and in the wide range of Scripture and subjects they address. They are singable by congregations. Much effort has gone into making sure they rhyme and fit the metre. They are refreshingly free of jargon. They are extremely varied, in number and length of lines per verse, and in ages included; some are written specifically for children. The Scripture and subject indexes in Chris's books are invaluable, making my task of selection much easier. I eagerly await each new composition.

Malcolm Jones, pastor, Elmstead Baptist Church, Kent

I have enjoyed singing Christopher Idle's hymns for over forty years—in them I know I will find robust theology, vivid biblical imagery, the careful crafting of metre and rhyme, and often the strong pairing of a text with a particular tune. It has been a delight to have regular opportunities to bring one or more of his wide-ranging hymns to the attention of ordinands, clergy or church musicians, through publication and at training events, with the aim of introducing more congregations to his fresh and striking turns of phrase.

Anne Harrison, freelance church musician and editor, Durham

The hymns in this book, as in Christopher Idle's two earlier collections, have a distinctive character. Like all good hymns, each has biblical content, a meaning which worshippers can confidently make their own. But what makes these texts attractively singable is that this writer also wrestles with form, how best to express in verse respectful of rhyme and metre (and in a variety of both) the content of the hymn. And there is something more: a controlled originality, self-effacing yet distinguishable, which marks this fine collection.

Bishop Timothy Dudley-Smith, hymnwriter, Salisbury

As chairman of the editorial board of the *Praise!* hymn-book published in 2000, I must take responsibility for the fact that this included more hymns from Chris Idle than from any other author; that says something for the value we placed upon the contemporary relevance, fine poetry and clear theology of Chris. A new collection of hymns and poems from the favourite hymnwriter of my mother, who greatly enjoyed reading and re-reading *Light upon the River* (1998), will be equally valued by many of us. Thank you, Chris.

Brian Edwards, pastor, writer, preacher; Surbiton, Surrey

*T*rees *along the* *R*iver

117 NEW HYMN AND SONG TEXTS 2008–2018,

WITH OTHER VERSES

BY CHRISTOPHER M IDLE

Dedicated to the memory of Edward Belsey (1917–2011) and George Wolf (1942–2016), dear Christian friends and church fellow-members at Bromley and Limehouse, who faced severe problems but who loved real hymns and hymn-books.

Published by Lost Coin Books
ISBN: 9781784984250
Printed in the UK by
and in the USA by Hope Publishing Company
Cover illustration by Hazel Voss

CONTENTS

CHRISTOPHER M IDLE

Christopher Martin Idle was born in Bromley Kent, in September 1938. After Eltham College he worked for three years in an office, a shop and then the hospital where he met Marjorie; they married in 1963. He studied English at St Peter's College, Oxford, and trained for ordination at Clifton Theological College, Bristol.

Then came thirty years in Anglican parish ministry, both urban and rural. A second spell in Peckham, SE London, ended soon after Marjorie's death from a brain tumour in 2003. Chris retired to a bungalow in Bromley, then in 2013 moved to a genuinely stunning 12th-floor flat in Herne Hill, SE24, not far from eldest son Timothy.

He joined Grace Church Dulwich (meeting in Rosendale Road School where his father Arthur belonged in 1916) and also attends St Paul's, Herne Hill (where his mother Kathleen was baptized in 1903). Chris has reluctantly given up football and early-morning jogging, but (often with family) watches Bromley and Barrow AFCs who have both won their respective leagues and Wembley trophies.

Previous hymn-collections (*Light upon the River* and *Walking by the River*) marked his 60th and 70th birthdays; since the latter in 2008 he has continued to write for several periodicals including *Churchman* (Church Society), *Evangelicals Now*, *New Directions*, the *Bulletin* of the Hymn Society of GB and Ireland and the Journal of the Prayer Book Society. He has contributed to the magisterial online *Canterbury Dictionary of Hymnology*, and still speaks occasionally on hymns, bravely on hymnbooks, and non-violently on issues of peace, war and Christian mission.

The present book is planned with Chris's 80th birthday in view. His four sons and their wives have families aged from two to eighteen; with his birth in SE London in 2016, Zachary Nathanael brought the total of grandchildren to a biblical twelve.

ON RIVERS, TREES AND WRITING

My next volume—should a next volume ever come to pass—may, I hope, show an improved tone of mind and feeling: but for the present, you must even accept the actual volume with all its shortcomings.

Christina G Rossetti, in a letter of 1862,
which I should have quoted in 2008.

I will praise God because of his word...In God's word will I rejoice.

Psalm 56:4, 10

Because you are my help, I sing in the shadow of your wings.

Psalm 63:7

I will praise God's name in song: and glorify him with thanksgiving.

Psalm 69:30

Then all the trees of the forest will sing for joy...

Psalm 96:12

Let the rivers clap their hands...let them sing before the LORD!

Psalm 98:8–9

Then they believed his promises: and sang his praise.   Psalm 106:12

Whoever is wise will ponder these things: and they shall understand the loving-kindness of the LORD.   Psalm 107:43

And the LORD God made all kinds of trees grow out of the ground—trees that were pleasing to the eye and good for food. In the middle of the garden were the tree of life and the tree of the knowledge of good and evil. A river watering the garden flowed from Eden; from there it was separated into four head-waters.

Genesis 2:9–10

Then they came to Elim, where there were twelve springs and seventy palm trees, and they camped there near the water.   Exodus 15:27

*...and [Solomon's] songs were 1,005; he spoke of trees, from the cedar that is in
Lebanon to the hyssop that grows out of the wall.*   1 Kings 4:32–33

*...like a tree planted by streams of water,
which yields its fruit in season
and whose leaf does not wither...*   Psalm 1:3

*...like a tree planted by streams of water
that sends out its roots by the stream.
It does not fear when heat comes;
its leaves are always green.*   Jeremiah 17:4

*Then he led me back to the bank of the river. When I arrived there, I saw a
great number of trees on each side of the river. He said to me, '...Fruit trees
of all kinds will grow on both banks of the river. Their leaves will not wither,
nor will their fruit fail. Every month they will bear, because the water from
the sanctuary flows to them. Their fruit will serve for food and their leaves for
healing.'*   Ezekiel 47:6–12

*Then the angel showed me the river of the water of life, as clear as crystal,
flowing from the throne of God and of the Lamb down the middle of the great
street of the city. On each side of the river stood the tree of life, bearing twelve
crops of fruit, yielding its fruit every month. And the leaves of the tree are for
the healing of the nations.*   Revelation 22:1–2

*I saw then that they went on their way to a pleasant river, which David the
king called the River of God, but John, the River of the Water of Life. Now their
way lay just upon the bank of the river; here therefore Christian and his com-
panion [Hopeful] walked with great delight; they drank also of the water of the
river, which was pleasant and enlivening to their weary spirits: besides, on the
banks of this river on either side were green trees, that bore all manner of fruit;
and the leaves of the trees were good for medicine; with the fruit of the trees
they were also much delighted; and the leaves they ate to prevent surfeits, and
other diseases that are incident to those that heat their blood by travels... Then
they sang...* John Bunyan, *The Pilgrim's Progress*, The First Part, 1678

By the time it came to the edge of the Forest the stream had grown up, so that it was almost a river...
> A A Milne, *The House at Pooh Corner*,1928, ch.6
> *see also Winnie the Pooh, 1926, chs.8 and 9*

Wood is a pleasant thing to think about. It comes from a tree, and trees grow, and we don't know how they grow. For years and years they grow, without paying any attention to us, in meadows, in forests, and by the side of rivers— all things one likes to think about...I like to think of the fish balanced against the stream like flags blown out; and of water-beetles slowly raising domes of mud upon the bed of the river. I like to think of the tree itself: first the close dry sensation of being wood; then the grinding of the storm; then the slow, delicious ooze of sap...The song of birds must sound very loud and strange in June; and how cold the feet of insects must feel upon it, as they make laborious progress up the creases of the bark, or sun themselves upon the great awning of the leaves...
> Virginia Woolf, *The Mark on the Wall*, a short story from 1917

Trees—a recurring fact of enjoyment all through my life...Trees are always the first things I seem to notice about places.
> Agatha Christie, *An Autobiography*, written 1950–65,
> published 1977

Writing is always about choosing what to leave out.
> David Jackman, 2012

The first lesson an author has to learn is that he cannot please everybody. P G Wodehouse, 1929

The mere act of writing opens up a gap between text and author... For George Herbert, to write poetry was to pray. Grace is built into his system; he takes it into church and then does battle with it. Kenneth Mason, c.2000

The days were not long enough as I found wonderful delight in meditating upon the depth of your design for the salvation of the human race. I wept at the beauty of your hymns and canticles, and was powerfully moved at the sweet sound of your church's singing. Those sounds flowed into my ears, and the truth streamed into my heart; so that my feeling of devotion overflowed, and the tears ran from my eyes, and I was happy in them.

Augustine of Hippo, Confessions, c.AD 400

As I went down to the river to pray...   African-American folk song

Where God doth dwell, sure heaven is there,
  and singing there must be;
since, Lord, thy presence makes my heaven,
  whom should I sing but thee?   John Mason, 1683

WARM THANKS

To all the people (see no.42), including many friends, whose comments have prompted these texts and/or helped to shape them for the better; to those gifted musicians and composers who have provided tunes; to my son Jonathan Idle for his proof-reading; to Michael Lin of West Norwood for the portrait on the back, and Hazel Voss of Staveley, Cumbria, for the brilliant cover picture of Kendal. Then crucially to Tim Thornborough, publisher of the earlier collections (1998 and 2008), for making this third one possible. The remaining errors, lapses, misjudgements etc are all my own work.

MILESTONES, SIGNPOSTS, COMPASS:
A MEMOIR, BY REQUEST
'WHY DO PEOPLE WRITE HYMNS?'

So enquired Paul Griffin (a 'librettist of sorts') in the Prayer Book Society's journal *Faith and Worship* for Easter 2010. He began with the dangers of showing off, while acknowledging that a painter enjoys creating a satisfying picture; but 'will wish that his [her] pleasure might be shared. So it is with hymnwriters; they may be writing for their own pleasure and for the worship of their Maker, but it would hardly be possible for them not to want their hymns to be sung, and duly credited.' Those last three words are more problematic; in a celebrity culture we sometimes wistfully recall an age where hymnwriters were anonymous, at least in their lifetime. So 'sung, and duly assessed' might be better; the strengths and (especially) weaknesses of a hymn cannot be fully appreciated until the singers are on their feet.

'Showing off', of course, can be a fault of writers, composers, musicians or singers. But Mr Griffin adds that 'hymns are a combination of words and music, and as long as each art observes just proportion, so that each can be enjoyed with rather than against the other, showing off is generally minimal'. So one hopes. It surely cannot be wrong—though it should be humbling—to enjoy words we have ourselves written, provided we don't imagine they were directly and divinely dictated (a fantasy still sometimes rearing its head). So long, too, as we can equally value the works of other writers, especially where our lives and efforts have intersected, as these pages will show.

A hymnwriter's life-story is not of itself one of sustained or repeated excitement. Some may have dramatic elements; the lives of Charles Wesley and John Newton come to mind, but Isaac Watts's career was fascinating rather than action-packed. Within living memory, Fred Kaan and Michael Saward survived sensational events not directly connected with their writing; other equally distinguished contemporary authors provide rather less matter for a biographer.

The writer of hymn texts has much in common with other authors, professional or not; we tend to work on our own, often from home and in 'spare' moments. The self-employed person has many freedoms but may also feel undervalued or insecure. I am not talking now about those whose real gifts lie in a musical direction, where the call of the stage, public platform or recording studio can be strong.

And John Calvin (quoted here at one remove) can join the greater number of those earlier writers to whom all present ones are indebted: 'Singing has the greatest value in kindling our hearts to a true zeal and eagerness to pray'; but 'We should be careful that our ears be not more attentive to the melody than our minds to the spiritual meaning of the words'. Over the centuries before and since, many have voiced similar concerns.

I have dared to suggest elsewhere that those mortals who are gifted equally in writing, composing, playing and singing are very few. Billy Joel may come to mind, such is God's 'common grace'; among Christians I can think of two, from Exeter and Glasgow respectively. I remain among those words-people who claim no expertise in any of the other three functions, and am privileged to know half a dozen living authors in a similar category. They follow the example of some of the great names among the classic hymnwriters. When others take over all four roles it is the words which tend to suffer, whether in rhyme, rhythm, grammar or even meaning.

In the face of the flood of singer-musician-composer-authors who currently dominate the charts, the shops and many of the churches, I am tempted to expand on a claim by the mathematical Cambridge Professor G H Hardy in 1941, 'The number of men who can do two things well is negligible'. He knew about numbers.

Those who labour for hours at a time in order to get a single line exactly right are, by and large, not much noticed by the wider church, let alone the world; we are mild eccentrics, simply distinguished from those with 'a proper job'. On a bad day, we may be interrupted in ways that would not happen in an office, shop, hospital or classroom (four venues where I have been employed in the past); after a bad night, no-one is ever much impressed when we fall asleep at a meeting the next morning.

That is not a complaint; this calling brings much enjoyment and occasional delight, gained from quarrying away prayerfully at a text with the help of our Bible, concordance, commentary, dictionary, thesaurus and other aids. The internet can now provide some of the help which many of us still enjoy getting from books.

And although I cannot speak for others, most of us have interests or occupations outside hymns, and find that one sphere of work happily and creatively overlaps with others. There is more to hymnwriting than meets the eye. By that I don't mean it is harder work than many imagine, though this is probably true, or should be. We work at different levels, all under the supreme aim, as we trust, of glorifying our God and Saviour. The immediate purposes will vary in scope; they may include meeting a need for a new book or 'hymn search'; a general invitation for a neglected topic; a personal request for a local event; or an inner compulsion to express a newly-found or rediscovered truth in a metrical form which others will want to sing. These aims may well intertwine or feed one another.

To say that such writing may also be a form of therapy, gratitude and prayer, is not to say that we do not need other forms of all three. Or our writing may be in part a protest against what we see as a fairly recent hostility to hymns. As the world is more hostile to the Christian gospel it is innately hostile to hymns expressing that gospel; even the best (unless they are critical or cynical about tradition) are often referred to with contempt. While some of them (old or new) no doubt deserve oblivion, when Watts or Wesley are scorned, ridiculed or omitted from verse anthologies, we suspect it is the subject-matter which proves unacceptable to committed unbelievers. The new secular 'inclusiveness' and 'toleration' clearly have their limits.

Even in today's churches, hymns in traditional form are either regarded as museum-pieces or (more likely) simply ignored because they are not known. The replacement of the hymn-book by the screen places more power than ever in the hands of the leadership or the musicians, taking it away from the congregation who could in the past at least see what they were missing. The reasons for this, and for the shift from supporting to performing, are complex; but there is certainly an uphill struggle to be faced.

One curiosity is repeated every December, when congregations and music groups who would normally be ashamed to be found singing anything as much as ten years old, suddenly switch to the nineteenth century and earlier to celebrate the birth of Christ, only to flick back to the latest 'hits' in January. That is why I am immensely grateful to the Hymn Society of Great Britain and Ireland, to Jubilate Hymns and Praise Trust, and for authors such as Prof J R Watson, for doing what they can to keep 'real hymns' in the public eye, and ear.

But much of this is general; I have been asked to tell my own story. So here is a related but more specific question: 'Are you still writing hymns?'

When *Walking by the River* was published for my 70th birthday in 2008 (following *Light upon the River*, 1998), I did not intend to add a further volume. When friends asked this further question, I would truthfully answer, 'Only when I am asked'—the rare exceptions being 'When I have to'!

MIXED FEELINGS
The enquiry arises sometimes out of compassion ('Still stuck in the same old rut?'), sometimes as a conversation-filler (like the weather), sometimes from genuine inter-

est. Other authors will know the mixed feelings the question evokes. I am inevitably reminded of the aged Oxford don who at high table at his college was placed next to the evening's guest, William Butler Yeats. 'He's a poet, you know', they helpfully explained beforehand. So over the soup, anxious to be the courteous host, the very senior academic opened with 'And are you still writing poetry, Mr Keats?'

A more personal pressure is that of time and age, as the years roll inexorably on. So many fine hymnwriters, not to mention the poets, have died while they seemed to have so much more to give; others have lived to fruitful age, into which (even if I survive) I do not intend to go on writing. My late friend Canon Michael Saward produced his definitive collection of 75 texts, named from his best-known 'Christ triumphant', for his seventy-fifth year; so I have cherished the hope of presenting a further 80 of mine for my eightieth. Perhaps inevitably, that number grew towards the hundred-plus which are now offered. This present, and my last, collection is as far as I shall get. So I have felt the pressure of bringing this book into its final shape, without (I hope) writing for the sake of writing.

In my twenties I presumed to emend a line of Wesley in a hymn that Marjorie and I chose for our wedding. Not then in the interests of more inclusive or updated language (that came later), but because this wedding hymn, while full of good things, sounded more of a negative note than seemed strictly desirable. It almost matched the seriousness of John Wesley's journal entry when Charles was married: 'solemn... dignity', etc.

Two years later came my ordination and a curacy in NW England, at Barrow-in-Furness in Cumbria. As told in *Light upon the River*, I overlapped briefly with my musically-gifted predecessor David Griffiths, who while we were together masterminded a memorable Youth Service at St Mark's Church. One tune he was keen to include needed some more usable words. 'You studied English', he said; 'Why don't you write something?'

Just twelve months earlier the aforementioned Billy Joel, known as a gifted sixteen-year-old musician, had a similar game-changing moment. The Long Island group he then played with needed more new material; 'What are you looking at me for?' said Billy. 'Well, you read a lot; you read a lot of books'. 'So what? That doesn't make me Robert Browning—or Bob Dylan'. 'Well', they said; 'give it a shot'. So he did; and so did I; the similarity ends there.

So my first original hymn texts featured at St Mark's, and I must have been sufficiently encouraged to attempt more. From 1966 onwards the million-selling *Youth*

Praise was making an impact in evangelical churches and youth groups nationwide; some three hundred of us celebrated a joyful 50th birthday in 2016. Editors Michael Baughen and Richard Bewes had not envisaged a sequel, but the first book had tapped into a richly creative vein, and in 1969 (by which time our family had moved to Peckham in SE London), *Youth Praise 2* was launched. Prompted by the new writing in YP1, I had sent a clutch of my Barrow hymns to Michael; and two of them became the joint firstfruits of my published hymnwriting. One was quite good and has sunk without trace; the other had major faults and has been much in demand.

I wrote to Michael again with two comments on YP2; one, critical of what I thought a mistaken inclusion (it could be sung only by white people); the other, in appreciation of its handful of Psalm versions, spearheaded by his own ground-breaking (if now overtaken) 'Blessed is the man'.

Because of this letter, or in spite of it, in early 1970 Michael invited me to join a small group compiling a more thorough collection of new Psalm versions and other Bible paraphrases which ultimately emerged in 1973 as *Psalm Praise*. The like-minded nature of the group was both a strength and a weakness; we were all young-ish white male evangelical Anglican clergy. This gave us a unity of understanding without having to argue over points of doctrine; but it also made for limitations in vision. Our senior member was Jim Seddon, an ever-gracious silver-haired former overseas mission-partner, 55 when we started work; while our acknowledged master in wordcraft was Timothy Dudley-Smith, then a mere 44 and already the author of his landmark metrical Magnificat, 'Tell out, my soul, the greatness of the Lord'.

Since at the time the *Psalm Praise* team members were seen as young upstarts, it is worth noting that they were to produce three bishops, two archdeacons, two canons, two prebendaries and various other notables.

But that is to look ahead; from the 1970s I was making the formative acquaintance of two more Michaels: Saward who had been my senior at school, and the younger Perry, whom I now met for the first time. The best work of this pair is to my mind quite outstanding; and 1970 marked the start of a close but feisty friendship, since the three of us were among the most committed writers during the years of compiling *Hymns for Today's Church* (1982, 2nd edition 1987).

The two Michaels and I would spark one another off in ways that were occasionally painful, often hilarious, sometimes highly creative. Others in the group (we worked on words, others on music) also provided great stimulus, but we became a distinctive trio. Michael Perry died aged 54 in 1995; Michael Saward, 82, in 2015; so they are not here to put their case. I had the sad privilege of preaching at the Tonbridge funeral of the younger one, and of writing obituaries for them both. But they have both gone into print with their stories, so I may be allowed to give mine. They both developed effective techniques for getting what they believed in; Perry by his charmingly persuasive skills, Saward by the art of eloquent filibuster. He would go on arguing his corner until we raised the white flag of surrender, simply to keep the agenda moving. But each of us respected, loved, commended and sometimes helped to fine-tune the writing of the other two. Please excuse the digression.

So forty-something years ago my own writing consisted partly of pre-1973 Psalm versions, then branching out into hymns (more rarely, songs) as we worked towards *HTC* and beyond. 'Jubilate Hymns' came into being in 1980, to formalise the practical arrangements; years later, Michael Saward wrote a breezy short history with his own recognisable slant on the facts.

GOING WEST

Meanwhile another landmark came in 1974, when George Shorney of Hope Publishing (USA) found himself singing our hymns on a visit to London, and included some of them in the first of many North American hymnals to feature our work. In subsequent years, our trio enjoyed in turn the lavish 'Hope' hospitality on various transatlantic visits, in return for lectures, presentations, and contributions to committees and hymn festivals. If our American friends had not yet faced up to the problems of archaic language, they were well ahead when it came to making texts more 'inclusive'—not exclusively masculine. So one reviewer of my 2008 collection *Walking by the River* complained about my use of 'Father', 'King' and 'Lord'; I might have responded by saying how convenient it would be to drop such titles and produce a greatly slimmed-down New Testament as a result.

But among happy friendships across the pond I count those of musician Donald Hustad (1918–2013) and the Canadian hymnwriter Margaret Clarkson (1915–2008), both of whom visited us more than once in England. I became acquainted with the fine work of North Americans such as Emily Brink, Carl Daw, Thomas Troeger and Jaroslav Vajda. My long-term membership of the North American Hymn Society came to an end only when its journal began publishing texts addressed to the 'Goddess of love'; one inclusive step too far? Those who are keenest to speak of 'God who is neither male nor female' usually end up with a feminine deity.

To step back again, Jim Seddon died at 69 (in 1983) and Michael Perry took the

'Jubilate' reins as our secretary with sometimes breathtaking energy. He was crucially supported by teams of helpers from the churches he served. Among several effective publications were *Church Family Worship*, and further Psalm and Carol books which were not best-sellers but which proved to be valuable resources.

Less successful was a 100-hymn Supplement to the 1965 *Anglican Hymn Book* (not from Jubilate); *Anglican Praise*, produced by Church Society and the Oxford University Press which I was persuaded to edit (with a team of five) in 1988. But neither of our parent bodies would or could do much to promote its use in the parishes.

Other editing work has included some glossy compilations for Lion Publishing in the 1980s, two enjoyable spells producing the quarterly *News of Hymnody* (1986–2002), and the *Bulletin* of the Hymn Society (more briefly, 2002–03). I mention this because over many years our work of writing and editing were interwoven. But inevitably there have been other landmarks. In 1984 I attended my first of many conferences of the Hymn Society of Great Britain and Ireland, several of which I shared with Marjorie up to 2002. These are great occasions of singing, but also of meeting other writers and composers, and a much wider range of hymnody than any one church can experience. They also stimulate more self-criticism and further writing as we become more aware of faults, gaps, needs, aspirations and possibilities.

FRIENDS AND FASHIONS
Many reasons to write will be apparent from the notes to the hymns which follow. Most elements of our historic creeds have been neglected at different periods, sometimes followed by an over-reaction as one or other doctrine comes to predominate. And the creeds do not deal with the earthly life and teaching of Jesus, nor with the changes in society which sometimes leave older hymns unused or unusable, and new ones essential. Timothy Dudley-Smith and Martin Leckebusch have proved stimulating companions here, while David Preston's Psalm paraphrases are unsurpassed. Hymn Society friends such as Robert and Jenny Canham, Elizabeth Cosnett, John Crothers, Edward Darling, Alan Gaunt, Anne Harrison, Elsabé Kloppers and Richard (Dick) Watson all add to the richness... but such lists are never complete.

Some church movements have focused overwhelmingly on individualistic and pietistic 'I/me' hymns or purely personal feelings; others are highly political but lose touch with their biblical roots; some use solely rural or western imagery. It has been easier in recent years to write hymns of protest than more positive national hymns; a self-consciously anti-establishment mood soon forms a 'liberal' but rather cynical establishment of its own, only for the pendulum to swing back in the next generation. Many writers try not to be carried away with the mood of the moment, while also responding to calls for new work on particular and contemporary needs.

One example of changing fashions: a cursory survey of hymns about loving God ('the first and great commandment') suggests a telling contrast. With some exceptions, up to about 1970 writers are in broad agreement about 'our love for him so faint and poor' ('and yet I want to love thee, Lord'—William Walsham How, 1872). One hundred years later a trickle of texts in the new mood soon became a flood, as congregations seemed keen to sing about how much (not how little) they love God (see the Hymn Society *Bulletin* no.257, June 2007). Such writers are rather less assured about how much they love their neighbours; that relative silence says it all. But is there no way of expressing our love for God without either unhealthy cringing or unconvincing self-promotion?

To revert to near where we started; the call to write hymns is a ministry in just as much need of prayer, toil, love, discipline, constant learning and humility, as any other. The fellowship and encouragement of a local church is one priceless essential. But while our singing together has been not only a blessing in praise of God, but also vital in spotting which texts and tunes have a future and which have not: to ask for prayer does not always come easily. To share with a church 'home group' the news that a manuscript is with the publisher, the proof-reading is going well, or a new hymn is causing problems, does not engender the same frisson of excitement as a prayer request for an evangelistic supper, a fresh recruit for SE Asia, a friend with terminal cancer, or a new baby. Perhaps that is as it should be; but many of God's quieter and longer-serving saints—I don't now mean writers!—remain in the background while others come and go with their welcomes and farewells.

NAMES AND NUMBERS

By the autumn of 2008 it seemed that I had enough hymns in the can, not yet taken out let alone sung, that it might not be a fruitful exercise to attempt more. But it should be apparent that, whatever my age or yours, hymns never need be in a rut. They are capable of almost infinite variety. Three months after my previous collection emerged, two men named Roger entered the story on the same November day. My vicar Roger Bristow (at Holy Trinity Church, Bromley Common) wanted to include an item of mine among the next month's carols; then my friend and fellow-Old-Elthamian Roger Scopes, a Minister in the United Reformed Church, telephoned to request a concluding carol on the theme of 'music' for the School Chapel service in four weeks' time.

My vicar may have hoped for something already in print; but I had not written many Christmas texts. How about a fresh approach specifically for my parish church, on the 'Trinity' theme which rarely features in carol services? But the school request was more urgent, and my first thoughts went down on paper that evening. I spent the next two days drafting and redrafting, and while working on the church carol (one line in particular), an idea arose suddenly for a quite different approach. So I was then occupied with three carols at the same time; all to be sung to familiar tunes, but music not completely 'owned' by traditional words. The first two tunes chose them-selves; so, by the end of that week, did the third.

Meanwhile, as it happened (and nothing is quite 'by chance'), Timothy Dud-ley-Smith telephoned me from Salisbury, and I made a flying visit to Wynne Bowen at Southsea. Both these long-time friends kindly agreed to look at what I had to offer to date, and under pressure of time made valuable comments. Although what I showed them was in each case about the tenth draft, all three needed a re-think at crucial points; see in this book nos.31 and 62. In the course of all this, the seeds of *Trees along the River* were planted. Maybe more requests would come in during what-ever time was left to me? This third collection had to be the 'river' again; Sold down the River, Old Man River…? Trees won in the end.

'When it hurts, we return to the banks of certain rivers'—so said Czeslaw Milosz, quoted by Robin Harvie in *Why We Run* (2011). On the same page, Harvie writes about running beside the Thames, 'with the sound of traffic muffled by the solid can-opy of leaves overhead', further upstream than I have gone but the same captivating river. And not only when it hurts!

Many pages could be taken up with trees in Scripture, trees I have loved or even climbed. In Baker's *Handbook of Bible Lists* (Grand Rapids, Michigan, 1981), its com-piler Andrew E Hill catalogues 24 Bible rivers, mostly by name, between Genesis 2 and Revelation 22. There is no specific list of trees, but among the 114 varieties of 'Old Testament Flora' and 48 New Testament species are of course many trees, from almond and aloe to walnut and wild olive. By 2017, the number of the world's tree-species had been calculated as 60,065.

And in the new creation, the new heaven and earth, will the trickling and ne-glected River Graveney (celebrated if not quite immortalised by the songs and CDs of my friend Arthur Kitchener) escape from its concrete cuttings in Streatham, or the

Effra from the hidden darkness of subterranean Herne Hill, to sunlit and tree-lined glories unimagined by our mortal minds? It is human, even creative, to speculate and wonder!

Will congregations take to new hymns? Some of them love new songs; and I often take heart from the words of the old music-hall singer Charlie Coburn: 'I sang my song to them, and they didn't like it. So I sang it again, and they still didn't like it. So I sang it a third time, and one of them thought he might just get to like it if I changed the tune and altered the words. So I sang it again, just exactly the same way, and after a bit they all liked it'.

Down to earth, now: Other differences from the earlier books will appear. This one gave up an attempt to find a round number of items; the first had 279, the second, 100 with two 'extras'. In spite of the superabundance of Christmas hymns and songs, more items for that season appear here than previously, nearly all in response to particular requests

I continue to be in debt to a huge galaxy of gifted friends; those whom death has taken include Donald Hustad, Michael Saward and Paul Wigmore. Many of the same group have helped enormously with both words and music; I name many of them in my earlier books. Among regular advisers, critics and encouragers, as well as some already mentioned, are Brian Edwards, Jonathan Gooch, David and Helen Hannant, Helen Hayward, Malcolm Jones, Sara Thomson and Noël Tredinnick. But I shall not attempt to list them all; simply remain glad for their gifts, achievements and friendships, past, present and (God willing) future. I am deeply moved by the fact that more than 250 tunes, many as yet unpublished, have been composed specifically for hymn-texts of mine; some have been acclaimed by well-qualified editors or other musicians as very fine. My regret is that, inevitably, some will never be sung or heard; I am no longer in a position to introduce new words, let alone music, to a Sunday congregation. In any case I am not the best judge of their lasting value.

One more exchange: TV writer David Quantick: 'Do you value the opinions of friends and family?' Film-maker John Panton: 'They provide brutally honest viewpoints—however upsetting. My wife is the best'.

Well, rarely quite brutal. But as I lived, wrote and sang for nearly ten years in the parish of Holy Trinity, Bromley Common, also joining in at the (Grace) Baptist Church in Hayes Lane before moving back to SE London in 2013 and joining Grace Church Dulwich: all glory be to the Three-in-One and One-in-Three, the Father, Son and Holy Spirit, for the joy of serving our one sovereign, holy God of grace, in writing, re-writing, singing and repeating his praise! Hallelujah!—and for now, Amen.

TEN FAQS: PEOPLE SOMETIMES ASK:

AREN'T YOU A MUSICIAN?
No. I can read a printed melody-line and pick it out on the keyboard, but not much more.

WHICH COMES FIRST, WORDS OR MUSIC?
It varies. I often write with a tune in mind, but this may not be the final choice of partner to the text. The notes with each item will illustrate some of the variety in this process.

DOES A HYMN TAKE LONG TO WRITE?
Again, variable. But I often scribble down a preliminary draft fairly quickly (hours rather than days); then it may take further weeks or months, including space for feedback, and need many more drafts as it is being crafted into an acceptable form. The final text is sometimes very different from the initial idea, and the recycling box soon fills up.

YOU SEEM TO LIKE RHYMING?
I try. But I don't often rhyme every line with a partner, as some very skilled writers do. I don't see rhyme as a burden but as a fruitful and satisfying discipline, helping us to sing and remember. It's a bit like the string round a parcel; without it, things can fall apart and make a mess.

WHAT'S YOUR FAVOURITE HYMN?
The 4th-century Latin *Te Deum Laudamus*, best known by its English version in the 1662 Book of Common Prayer, 'We praise thee, O God; we acknowledge thee to be the Lord'. But if you mean a metrical hymn in a regular pattern of rhyming verses then 'Hark, the herald angels sing' (preferably at least four stanzas), as traditionally revised from Charles Wesley's 1738 original.

WHO IS YOUR FAVOURITE HYMN-WRITER?
Isaac Watts (1674–1748). Ann Griffiths (1776–1805) is incomparable, but more lim-

ited and not very accessible, even in translation. But several contemporary favourites include Timothy Dudley-Smith and Thomas Troeger.

WHAT'S THE DIFFERENCE BETWEEN HYMNS AND SONGS?

They overlap quite a bit. But the words of hymns (e.g. 'Love divine', 'Rock of ages') may be sung to more than one tune, usually composed by someone other than the author. Sometimes a new tune can breathe life into familiar words. Most hymns have two or more matching verses in a regular pattern. A hymn is best sung once only, and not followed immediately by another hymn. Songs may be more personal and presented by a soloist or group; hymns are for the whole congregation.

ARE HYMNS POETRY?

Yes, in a specialised (not inferior!) genre. Poets and songwriters may write first to please or express themselves; hymnwriters must have a (varied) congregation in mind, as servants of the church as well as of the word of Scripture.

WHAT WOULD YOU SAY TO A BUDDING OR ASPIRING HYMNWRITER?

Write to me (with old-style s.a.e.) for a copy of Hints to Hymnwriters—which also recommends other matter for reading and action.

HOW IS A HYMN-BOOK PUT TOGETHER?

Actually, not many people ask this. Those who do may consult the website of the Hymn Society of GB and Ireland, '80 Treasures'; under the 1990s is Treasure No.62. Many other delights await them here.

If these Q&As and other matters touched on above ring a bell, you may have been reading *A Functional Art*, Timothy Dudley-Smith's *Reflections of a Hymn Writer* (2017). I hope so. But the present book was virtually complete before I read his characteristic masterpiece; a vital landmark, even in the 1% where we don't see things in quite the same way! Please also see my Appendix E.

PERMISSIONS AND COPYRIGHTS

If the suggested tune is not readily available, please consult the author at:

christophermidle@gmail.com

or 50 Park View House, Hurst Street, Herne Hill, London SE24 0EH—also giving a postal address. For permission to reprint in the UK (other than for occasional or one-off use) please contact **Jubilate Hymns Ltd**, www.jubilate.co.uk; Email: copyrightmanager@jubilate.co.uk. In the footnotes to the hymns, 'TAG' refers to the Text Advisory Group of Jubilate Hymns.

But if **Praise Trust** appears under the item, you will need The Copyright Manager, Praise Trust, 7 Arlington Way, London EC1R 1XA. Email: admin@praise.org.uk.

In the USA: Hope Publishing Co, 380 South Main Place, Carol Stream, IL 60188 (Email: hope@hopepublishing.com)

For all other countries, please refer to Jubilate Hymns.

Texts are also part of the CCL Licensing Scheme; some appear on the Jubilate or Praise websites; my warm thanks to my J and P friends for their patience, encouragement and efficiency.

HYMNS THROUGH
THE BIBLE

Genesis 1:1–2:4 (one)
Beginnings—1

1   FIRST GOD SAID, LET THERE BE LIGHT

1   First God said, Let there be light!
With the angels let us sing:
made and named the day and night;
praise to our Creator-King!

2   Formed a great expanse on high…
tamed the waves beneath the sky…

3   God created sea and land…
green things grow by God's command…

4   Sun and moon and every star…
shine immeasurably far...

5   Fishes swarm in all the seas…
birds hatch out among the trees…

6   All earth's creatures God designed…
crowned the work with humankind…

7   Then most holy and most blessed…
dawned the Sabbath of God's rest…

Praise Trust.   77 77
Tune: CREATOR-KING, by Gill Berry (2012); or MONKLAND

Scriptures: Gen 1:1–2:4
Written: Bromley, Kent, January 2011
First published: *Evangelicals Now,* October 2012
While preparing for a 'Messy Church' talk on creation, at Holy Trinity Church, Bromley Common, I realised that we lacked a text about the seven days of Genesis chapters 1–2. Although we did not launch the hymn in that brief event, it remained as a resource for adult occasions.

Genesis 1:1–2:4 (two)
Beginnings—2

2   GOD SAID FIRST, LET THERE BE LIGHT

1   God said first, Let there be light!
        God made all things good;
    made and named the day and night,
        made them by his word.

By the word of God it has all been made;
    everything good, very very very
    good good:
God said first, Let there be light:
    God made all things good.

2   Then God formed a dome on high…
        tamed the waves beneath the sky…

3   God created land and sea…
        fruit and flower, grass and tree…

4   Sun and moon and all the stars…
        Venus, Mercury and Mars…

5   Fishes swimming in the seas…
        birds to fly among the trees…

6   Then came creatures great and small…
        man and woman care for all…

7   And the seventh day God blessed…
        holy Sabbath, day of rest…

Tune: OLD MACDONALD

Scriptures: Gen 1:1–2:4

Written: Bromley, Kent, Jan 2011

This was written and launched in 'Messy Church' at Holy Trinity Bromley Common (see no.1) in January 2011, revised from a 1990s version introduced at Pilgrims' Way Primary School in the Old Kent Road. Our theme was the Creator and the days of creation in the book of Genesis; I also drafted a different chorus for every stanza, but decided this made it too complicated.

Genesis 1 and beyond
Beginnings—3

3 EACH NEW DAY AND DAWNING SPRING

1 Each new day and dawning spring,
    earth is given
all that God delights to bring:
    gifts from heaven.
One Creator, Lord of all
    works uncounted,
forms their beauty, vast or small,
    scale unbounded.

2 Every month and all the weeks,
    it is written,
come from God, the Lord who speaks
    to a pattern.
Turquoise, crimson, purple, green,
    land and ocean,
silver, gold and rainbows shine
    through creation.

3 Evening, morning, noon and night,
    never ceasing,
all are open to God's sight
    and his blessing.
As each date and day and hour
    time is turning,
so his wisdom, love and power
    give it meaning.

4 Though our sin brings slavery,
    death and ruin,
God can cancel what would be
    our undoing.
Evil is our present foe,
    spoiling, wrecking;
God has purposed long ago
    our remaking.

5 Father, Holy Spirit, Son:
    praise their splendour!
Glory, good and grace are one
    in their grandeur.
All our time is from the Lord,
    faithful Giver;
trust his truth, obey his word,
    new for ever.

7474D Tune: GWALCHMAI

Scriptures: Gen 1   Rom 8:18–23
Written: Thrandeston and Wortham, Suffolk; Herne Hill, SE London: March 2017
Near the time of going to press I decided to replace another children's song with this hymn. Prompted by both rural and urban scenery, it reaches well beyond the opening pages of Genesis but stays rooted in the creation narrative. True rhyme alternates here with half-rhyme or assonance in the even-numbered lines.

Genesis 1:11–13

Just trees

4 HOW WE PRIZE THE GIFT OF TREES

1 How we prize the gift of trees,
God be praised for such as these:
beauty of the vale and hill,
wood for human craft and skill.

2 Wood for ark that rode the flood,
doorposts marked with sheltering
    blood;
roof-beams at Jerusalem,
manger-bed in Bethlehem.

3 Boats of every shape and size,
noble ships of merchandise;
boat for Jonah's speedy doom;
ships transporting Paul to Rome.

4 Shepherd's staff to guide the sheep,
fishing-boat with Christ asleep;
wood of sycamore and vine,
table set for bread and wine.

5 Then the garden, Christ is there;
olive trees observe his prayer;
soon the soldiers' clubs and swords;
find the triumph is the Lord's.

6 See the cross-beam, drenched with
    blood
of the eternal Son of God;
from such vileness and such wood,
God has brought eternal good.

7 Tree of judgement, tree of grace,
tree of life for all our race;
as from cedar, oak and plane,
hope and green can spring again.

8 Where the heavenly rivers flow
leaf and fruit for ever grow;
God has planted every tree;
praise his name eternally.

77.77 Tune: INNOCENTS or VIENNA

Scriptures: Gen 1:11-13; 2:8-17; 3:22; 6:11-14; 18:1   Exod 12:1-13   1 Kgs 5:1-9; 6:9-18   Ezra 3:7   Ps 23:4   Ezek 27   Jonah 1:1-3   Mark 4:35-38; 14:12-26   Luke 2:7; 19:4; 22:39; 23:26-33   John 15:1-5; 18:1-11   Acts 2:23-24; 27:1–28:14   Rev 2:7; 22:1-2,14

Written: Herne Hill, SE London, 2nd Dec 2015

Most of my dozen homes have had at least one tree in the garden; a rich variety in Suffolk, and from 2013 a view of hundreds from my 12th-floor windows. I have always loved trees: for climbing, goalposts or wickets; shelter, shade and fruit; animal, bird and insect life; landmarks and sheer beauty, even firewood. This hymn reflects some of their biblical significance; most dreadful yet most dear is surely the tree of 1 Peter 2:24.

Genesis 1:20–28 (one)

All creatures great

5   GOD'S CREATURES FROM THE DEPTHS UKNOWN

1   God's creatures from the depths
        unknown
    with which the seas are swarming
    make music of their very own,
    and dances for performing.
        Beyond all human skill
        they keep their secrets still;
        when they become our friends
        we start to make amends
    for all the grief we bring them.

2   And monsters tread among the trees
    or roam the wide savannah;
    we hear the voice of such as these
    and catch their loud hosanna.
        If humbly we can learn
        that trust is what we earn,
        then we shall never need
        the policies of greed
    which hunt them to extinction.

3   And birds which soar through open
        skies,
    great wingspans of high heaven:
    they too can serve to make us wise
    with minds that God has given.
        Within a Father's care
        they rule the upper air;
        to watch them in the wild
        we wonder like a child,
    and bow before their Maker.

4   Yet, Lord, we see your truest face,
    your true but wounded image,
    in human beings, honoured race,
    with our eternal lineage.
        So let us never spoil
        the air, the sea, the soil;
        your likeness, Lord, restore
        in us, to love you more
    and treasure all creation.

8787 6666 7   Tune: EIN' FESTE BURG

Scriptures: Gen 1:20–28   Job 40:15–41:34   Ps 69:34; 104:21–26; 107:23–24; 148:7–13   Jonah 1:17
Matt 6:26; 12:40
Written: Herne Hill, SE London, 1–19 Sept 2016
This began with the amazing sea creatures of whom I had been reading, in a history of 'Greenpeace' by its
co-founder Robert Hunter. The text then grew to include earth, sky, and the human beings who were made
to rule God's world. A large theme seemed to require a large tune, for which I had written only once before.

Genesis 1:20–28 (two)
All creatures small and very small

6   GOD'S SMALLEST CREATURES THRIVE

1 God's smallest creatures thrive
in billions yet unknown;
by his first blessing they survive,
and by his will alone.

2 In water, earth or air,
each in its own abode,
their life is needed everywhere
and all are known to God.

3 Such miniatures so small,
escaping human sight,
are marvels as they swim or crawl,
and miracles of flight.

4 Their life-span may be brief,
unnoticed for their size,
but science based on true belief
can spring untold surprise.

5 Each masterpiece so frail,
each new-discovered skill:
while earth shall last, they will not fail
to serve their purpose still.

6 Your praise shall never end,
Creator of us all,
who planned that we should all depend
upon the very small.

SM   Tune: FRANCONIA or VENICE

Scriptures: Gen 1:20–25   Ps 78:45–46; 104:24–25; 105:30–35   Matt 10:29–30   Luke 12:6
Written: Herne Hill, SE London, 9–19 Sept 2016
Having just written (no.5) about the largest creatures, I thought it good to turn my attention to the smallest; a short metre for tiny things.

Genesis 2:4–9

More trees, or fewer? A conservation hymn

7 WHEN GOD MADE ALL THINGS WELL

1 When God made all things well
and trees adorned the earth,
how few at first could tell
their beauty or their worth;
     but cedar, pine
     and olive wood
     are still a sign
     of all that's good.

2 When forests are cut down
and greed becomes our goal,
where green is turned to brown
and deserts take control;
     what evils come,
     and harm untold
     to this our home,
     our precious world.

3 Our sinful heart rebels
against the laws you give;
God save us from ourselves,
that we repent and live.
     May humankind
     give earth its due
     till woodlands find
     their life made new.

4 Before new poisons reign
or earth and waters choke,
let us with zeal regain
the palm, the beech, the oak;
     here as in heaven
     your will be done,
     and thanks be given
     to you alone.

6666 4444 Tune: ST JOHN

Scriptures: Gen 1:11-12; 2:8-9   Isa 2:12-17   Zech 11:2   Matt 6:10   Rom 8:18-21
Written: Herne Hill, SE London, 1–3 Dec 2015.
See also the notes to No.4: the way we treat our trees now has huge significance for humanity and planet earth.

Genesis 2:4–14

Trees, rivers, people—and God

8   TREES ALONG THE RIVER

1 Trees along the river,
sunshine on our way;
wind across the hilltop,
sea and sand and spray:
  rain for thirsty pastures,
  scenes of green or blue,
  every brilliant rainbow
  shows us something new.

2 Streams that bless our cities
bring us countless joys;
trees give shade and beauty
under changing skies:
  neighbours bear God's image,
  none beyond his care;
  earth is filled with glory
  shining everywhere.

3 To the river Jordan
Jesus came for us,
but a fiercer torrent
met him at the cross;

on that tree he suffered
as the Scriptures said,
all the waves of judgement
pouring on his head.

4 Hidden needs or open.
found in every place –
some who cry for mercy,
all in need of grace:
  bring, Lord, that refreshing
  which you love to give,
  lead us to that river
  where we drink, and live!

5 God among your people,
Christ who knows us all,
Spirit of renewal,
make us hear your call!
  God of towns and nations,
  river, wind and wave,
  challenge, choose and change us,
  show your power to save!

Praise Trust 6565D Tune: EVELYNS or GOSHEN

Scriptures: Gen 2:8–14 Exod 15:27 Num 33:9 Ps 1:3 Jer 17:7-8 Ezek 47:1-12 Rev 22:1–2
Written: Bromley, Kent and local travels, April and July 2012.
In the case of 'As the light upon the river', the 1998 book title was taken from the hymn text. With this it was the other way round; I had chosen a provisional title for my third collection of texts (following *Walking by the River*, 2008), and wondered if a new hymn could begin with that phrase. There are many riverside trees in Scripture—and our cities as well as our countryside.

Genesis 2–3

Adam, Christ and us

9 ADAM CHOSE REBELLION

1 Adam chose rebellion;
   we have done the same:
   outcast till we're rescued,
   trusting Jesus' name.

2 In his grace abounding
   through the ages long,
   God in mercy meets us,
   gives us his new song.

3 If a second Adam
   had not come to save,
   we would all have perished
   in a hopeless grave.

4 Blessed be God—for Jesus
   stood where Adam fell!
   Blessed are all who love him,
   our Emmanuel!

6565   Tune: CASWALL, or a new tune

Scriptures: Gen 2–3   Rom 5:12–21   1 Cor 15:21–23; 44–49
Written: Herne Hill, SE London, 27–29 December 2016
Thanks mainly to some haunting newer music, the quaint medieval carol 'Adam lay ybounden' has become an almost obligatory choir item at many traditional Christmas carol services. But can we do better with the words, which are neither biblical nor very intelligible? It seemed worth a try; this short hymn uses some of the same themes and sound-patterns, but its more regular metre probably needs a new and more sharply-edged tune than most of the gentle 6565s. This was among my final entries for the present book.

Genesis 3
The fallen creation

10   THE CRUELTIES OF NATURE, LORD

1 The cruelties of nature, Lord,
   we find so hard to take;
   was it for this you fashioned all
   that you delight to make?

2 When neither bright nor beautiful
   your creatures stalk their prey,
   a food-chain full of blood and death
   with mercy far away?

3 And yet our choices also lead
   to spreading grief and pain,
   and humans have become their cause
   by reckless greed of gain.

4 Once free, now fallen and corrupt,
   our innocence has gone;
   our sickness now infects the world
   and makes the earth to groan.

5 The waves and fires that wreck our homes,
   the spreading desert sands,
   the dying species, are the work
   of human brains and hands.

6 We multiply the means of death
   which cannot draw a line
   between the evil and the good,
   whatever our design.

7 Our God, we need your mighty arm
   to move our heart and mind;
   if we would heal our wounded earth,
   Lord, heal all humankind.

CM Tune: BANGOR

Scriptures: Gen 3   Rom 8:18–25
Written: Herne Hill, SE London, 12–14 Sept 2016
Having written recently and positively about all creatures great and small, I thought it right to reflect the downside of the natural (or unnatural) world, and the destruction and disasters for which we humans are largely responsible.

Genesis 9:12–17

All the colours of the rainbow

11 ALL COLOURS IN THE RAINBOW SHINE

1 All colours in the rainbow shine;
  we see, and we have heard
  the promise coupled with the sign:
  our God will keep his word.

2 Gold is the colour of the sun
  and silver are the stars;
  they praise the High and Holy One,
  their First and final Cause.

3 Green is the colour of the trees,
  of pasture, plant and leaf:
  with green, the fruits of earth increase;
  without it, all is grief.

4 Blue is the colour of the skies,
  and blue the sunlit sea
  where wind and wave obey his voice:
  the Lord of Galilee.

5 Brown is the colour of the wood
  when carpentry supplies
  untold disgrace, eternal good:
  the cross where Jesus dies.

6 Red is the colour of his blood,
  the colour of our sin;
  without that blood, we never could
  be clean from stain within.

7 Purple, the colour of a king,
  the robe they made him wear;
  they mocked him then, but now we sing
  his reign is everywhere.

8 All colours blend in heaven's gems
  beyond our earthly gaze:
  a city rich in diadems
  for Christ's eternal praise.

CM Tune; NATIVITY

Scriptures: (all) Exod 25:1-7 1 Tim 6:17 (verse 1) Gen 9:12-17 (2) Gen 12:14-19 (3) Gen 1:11-13
Ps 23:2 Mark 6:39 (4) Gen 1:6-9 Ezek 1:26 Mark 4:35-41 (5) Mark 15:21-39 Acts 5:30 1 Pet 2:24 (6)
Isa 1:18 Eph 1:7 (7) Matt 28:16-20 John 19:1-3 1 Cor 15:24-25 (8) Rev 21:19-21
Written: 27-29 Nov 2015, mainly while revisiting Suffolk. A friend suggested that this was more a poem
than a hymn. So be it; but some poems have been set to music too. I am not the first to write of biblical
colours.

Genesis 17:1–8

Singing with saints and angels

12   I LONG TO SING WITH ABRAHAM

1 I long to sing with Abraham
the father of us all
who trust the promise of the Lord,
and follow at his call.
I long to sing with Miriam
as Israel's host walks free,
when music sounds along the shore
and echoes by the sea.

2 I long to sing with Deborah,
God's justice coming near;
of quaking mountains, rushing streams
and faith replacing fear.
I long to sing with Naomi,
with Boaz and with Ruth,
the tunes of harvest and of home,
Christ's family, God's truth.

3 I long to sing with Samuel
whose mother sang before;
their words have lasted to this day,
their prayers for evermore.
I long to sing with Daniel
who prays with faithful friends,
and never wavers from his Lord
no matter what he sends.

4 I long to sing with Simeon
and Mary, young and old,
of peace, salvation, glory, light
for Israel and the world.
I long to sing with Lazarus,
and what a song is his,
raised from the tomb, but first to touch
the very edge of bliss!

5 I long to sing with Barnabas,
Priscilla, Silas, Paul;
with Luke and Mark,
   whose second chance
spells mercy for us all.
I long to sing with Timothy
in Philippi or Rome,
with Peter in proud Babylon,
on travels far from home.

6 I long to sing with Gabriel
and all the heavenly host
at our Creator's glorious throne,
his love our only boast.
I long to sing with all the saints,
the leaders and the led,
and with the Lord of all the songs,
Redeemer, King and Head.

CMD   Tune: FOREST GREEN

Selected Scriptures: (verse 1) Rom 4:16–17 Exod 15:19–21 (2) Judg 5 Ruth 4:13–22 (3) 1 Sam 3:19
Dan 2:17–23 (4) Luke 2:25–35 John 12:1–2 (5) Acts 16:25 1 Pet 5:12–13 (6) Rev 4 and 6.
Written: Herne Hill, SE London, March 2016
A text which began with Lazarus, prompted by a Holy Week reading, and grew backwards to Abraham
and forwards to heaven.

Genesis 39:20–23

By faith

13   FAITHFUL JOSEPH

1   Faithful Joseph…
      trusted God…
   even in the prison…
      God was there…

2   Lonely Hannah…
      trusted God…
   after all her crying…
      she found joy…

3   Brave old Daniel…
      trusted God…
   in the den of lions…
      he was safe…

4   Good Queen Esther…
      trusted God…
   came into the kingdom…
      just in time…

5   When there's trouble…
      trust in God…
   Jesus will be with you…
      he's the King…

Praise Trust   Tune: FRÈRE JACQUES

Scriptures: Gen 39:20–23   1 Sam 1:1–2:10   Esther, esp. ch.4   Ps 37:3   Prov 3:5–6   Dan 6
Matt 28:20   Acts 17:7

Written: Bromley, Kent, October 2012

The 'Messy Church' theme at Holy Trinity Bromley Common that month was the story of Esther. One challenge was to simplify the events without distorting the drama; another was to find something to sing. So I offered two verses (4 and 5 above) for the afternoon of 21st October, accompanied by Johnny Gooch on Kate Hircock's accordion, and sung as a round (in two groups; given more time we might have had four) with each line repeated.

Did Esther trust God? Famously, she is the heroine of a book where the divine name does not directly appear. But I take 4:15–16 (they fasted) to indicate prayer as well. The launch of this little song happened to come in our Queen Elizabeth's Diamond Jubilee year; the parallels and contrasts were a useful aid. But later I recognised that Esther needed company and could well be joined by some other Bible characters (NB, two male, two female).

Genesis 50:20
The greatest text?

14 THE STORY OF JOSEPH, THE FAVOURITE SON

1 The story of Joseph, the favourite son,
  a household divided, and shameful things done:
  by faith it is written, by faith understood:
  they meant it for evil; God meant it for good.
  Their plots to do murder, their quarrels and strife,
  God used for his purpose, the saving of life.

2 The story of Adam, humanity's fall,
  of Abraham, Isaac and Jacob and all:
  of villains in palaces, prophets in caves,
  of Israel in Babylon, exiles and slaves:
  by faith it is written, by faith understood:
  they meant it for evil; God meant it for good.

3 The story of Jesus, his death on a cross,
  betrayal, denial, the ultimate loss;
  the hands of the wicked who set up the tree
  and nailed up God's Son, for all nations to see:
  by faith it is written, by faith understood:
  they meant it for evil; God meant it for good.

4 Far more than a story, eternal good news;
  no future in blaming the Gentiles or Jews:
  what would we have done at that time, in their place?
  But in the shed blood is our hope, by his grace.
  Unmeasured his wisdom, unfathomed his ways;
  for such great salvation, to God be all praise!

11 11 11 11 11 11 new tune needed

Scriptures: Gen 50:20   1 Kings 18–19   Neh 13:2   2 Chron 36   John 19:16–20
Acts 2:22–24   Rom 11:33–36   Eph 1:3–12
Written: Herne Hill, SE London, 8 Nov 2015

This foundational Bible text seems to sum up not only the career of Joseph, son of Jacob, but the entire Old Testament history. It then forms the perfect bridge to the New Testament, leading inevitably and explicitly to the cross, as explained and preached by the apostle Peter on the day of Pentecost (Acts 2). A hymn expressing something of this mystery of providence and grace seemed long overdue.

Exodus 1–3

At work

15 GIVE THANKS FOR THOSE WORKING

1 Give thanks for those working
   to serve one another
   in time and in talents
      with God-given powers;
   the work of our Maker
   will daily sustain us;
   the call is the Lord's and
      the calling is ours.

2 The work of the midwives
   ensured the survival
   of Israel in Egypt,
      the people of God;
   the work of a shepherd
   entrusted to Moses
   to lead through the desert
      where angels had trod.

3 The work of the weavers,
   designers and craftsmen,
   constructed the dwelling
      where God was made known;

   pure gold and bright silver,
   blue, purple and scarlet,
   in beauty of holiness
      Christ is foreshown.

4 The work of a joiner,
   a carpenter-builder,
   brought touches of heaven
      to service on earth;
   and tent-making, trading,
   and farming and fishing,
   all found new dimensions
      because of new birth.

5 The work of a Saviour,
   to open a kingdom
   is ours at the cost of
      his body and blood;
   for none could redeem us,
   no helper but Jesus;
   all praise to the Worker
      who brings us to God.

6665D (12 11 12 11)   new tune needed

Scriptures: Exod 1–3; 35–40 Matt 4:18–22; 26:26–29   Mark 6:3;   Acts 16:11–15; 18:1–3 1 Pet 3:18; 4:10
Written: Herne Hill, SE London, April 2016.
Arising from my own Bible-reading in Exodus, this is another attempt to reduce the large gap in hymns about work; see also nos.27 and 28. Among professions specifically noted here, Terri Coates has recently found that 'midwives are virtually non-existent in literature' (*Midwives Journal*, Jan 1998). All honour then to the late Michael Hewlett for his Christmas song, 'When God almighty came to be one of us' (1969), which has 'Sing all you midwives, dance all the carpenters…'. In 1963 I married a midwife; eleven months later we needed one. Some textual changes (including a new first line) were made by Jan 2017 in response to friendly comments.

Exodus 2:1-2

Out of Egypt

16   BY THE RIVER, THAT OLD NILE RIVER

1   By the river, that old Nile river,
there floats a bundle; and now, whoever
would guess what's in it?
A little baby; asleep!

2   By that river comes Pharaoh's daughter;
she sees that bundle, and from the water
they take that baby,
that little baby to keep!
 Come along to hear my song;
 sing how the Lord makes the weak ones strong.
 Trust in God, don't be sad;
 see how the Lord brings good from bad:

3   From that river the baby Moses
is taken care of, until he chooses;
and God sends Moses
to set the Israelites free.
 Come along to hear my song;
 sing how the Lord makes the weak ones strong.
 Trust in God, don't be sad;
 see how the Lord brings good from bad:

4   Out of Egypt, beyond old Moses,
another baby, whose name is Jesus
was sent to free us:
the whole world's Saviour is he!

Tune: OLD MAN RIVER

Scriptures: Gen 50:20 Exod 2:1-10; 3:7-10 Matt 2:13-15 John 4:42 Heb 11:24-25
2 Cor 12:9-10 1 John 4:14
Written: SE London (Peckham and Herne Hill), 2000–2015
Most fitting, I hope, for the present book and its title, here is another song from Exodus, and another river to add to the list in *Walking by the River* (2008). Musical purists may complain that the text does not use all of the tune—or that it presumes to use it at all. All I can claim is that there are precedents, and that it is a singable and creative use of a very fertile Scripture narrative.

Exodus 3:10

True shepherds

17 AMONG THE SHEEP GOD MEETS HIM

1 Among the sheep God meets him,
   the stranger with a past;
but stranger things are coming:
a bush on fire, an angel,
a voice calls 'Moses, Moses!',
   rescue has come at last.

2 Among the sheep they find him.
   the boy who will be king;
the youngest son of Jesse
is summoned and anointed;
he has the gift of music:
   David can play and sing.

3 Among the sheep we see them;
   the shepherds in the night,
who in a sudden brightness
hear news of Christ, a Saviour,
a baby in a manger:
   Bethlehem filled with light.

4 The chief of all the shepherds,
   the Rescuer, the Way:
the greater far than Moses,
the promised Son of David,
the song of our salvation:
   Jesus is Lord today!

767776 new tune needed

Scriptures: Exod 3:1-10 1 Sam 16 Luke 2:1-20 John 10:11; 14:6 1 Pet 5:4
Written: Herne Hill, SE London, August 2015
My preparation to preach at Holy Redeemer Church, Streatham (12th July 2015, and see nos.102 and 114), on 1 Samuel 16, where David the future king is twice found with the sheep, led back in time to Moses and forward to the Lord Jesus, for other shepherds and different flocks.

Exodus 4:22–23

Freedom song

18 LET MY PEOPLE GO

1 'Let my people go'
is the summons of the Lord;
spoken to the lords of earth
who rule by chain and sword.
'Let my people go',
the repeated, urgent call;
yet so many hearts are hard
and do not heed at all.

2 'Let my people go',
for they truly are his own;
chosen, called, the firstborn son
eternally foreknown.
'Let my people go
so that they may all serve me';
once this people found escape
from terror, through the sea.

3 'Let my people go';
they are purchased with a price:
rescued by a life laid down,
the blood of sacrifice.

'Let my people go';
some still long to be set free:
so we cry to God to save
and bring full liberty.

4. 'Let my people go';
let the world now hear God's voice;
giving justice, keeping faith
with people of his choice.
'Let my people go',
brothers, sisters, pray through pain
for their freedom, shelter, hope;
with them we plead again.

5 'Let my people go':
words that soon will be no more,
when God's universe, in Christ
shall worship and adore.
'Let my people go';
then the ending of the night,
when creation is renewed
in resurrection-light!

Praise Trust 5776D (distinctive) new tune needed

Scriptures: Exod 4:22–23; 5:1 etc   Rom 8:18–21   1 Cor 6:20; 7:23   1 Pet 1:18–19   2 Pet 3:13
Written: Herne Hill, SE London, February 2016
When two separate Bible-reading plans converged for me, I was struck by the insistent repetition of this four-word summons: 'Let my people go'—seven occurrences of God's demand to Pharaoh through Moses. They are also well known from the spiritual 'Go down, Moses', which does not get as far as '…that they may serve me'. But maybe there is room for a more contemporary treatment, repeating more explicitly the need for freedom today, in many modern 'Egypts'.

Exodus 20:21

Darkness

19   IN THE DARKNESS WHERE GOD WAS

1   In the darkness where God was,
Moses in time past drew near;
bold to listen then, because
God is speaking; man must hear.

2   In the darkness where we hide
all earth's sunlight soon grows dim:
it was dark when Jesus died,
never need we hide from him.

3   In the darkness where we weep
Lord, be our companion still,
night or morning, wake or sleep;
you have wept; we fear no ill.

4   In the darkness where we grieve
in the shadow of the grave,
Lord, be with us; we believe
you are risen, you will save.

5   Darkness will not, cannot last:
you have kept us in your sight,
known our sorrows, held us fast;
shone in us eternal Light.

7777   Tune: HEINLEIN or ST BEES

Scriptures: Exod 10:21–23; 20:21   Deut 4:11–14   Psalm 23:4   Mark 15:33-34   John 3:19   1 John 1:5
Written: Herne Hill, SE London, 24-25 Jan 2016
Prompted by a sermon on another part of the story of Moses, and reflecting on a single text (Exodus 20:21) which had often intrigued and moved me.

Exodus 33–34
The Law and the Gospel

20 GOD OF ALL SPEECH, GOOD AND TRUE

1 God of all speech, good and true,
law and gospel come from you;
in whatever time or place
every Scripture shows your grace,
light to guide our wayward race.

2 Moses climbs the mountain peak,
summoned there to hear you speak;
hidden safe within the rock,
conscious of his waiting flock,
sheltered from the thunder-shock:

3 Stands alone beneath the sky,
sees your glory passing by;
here is written by your hand
every word of your command,
so that all can understand.

4 Showing mercy as you choose,
none in need will you refuse;
yet your wrath will surely fall
on the fools who mock your call,
think themselves the lords of all.

5 Holy Father, we have now
no more need of Sinai's brow,
no more sacrifice or blood;
Christ for us went through the flood,
brought us near to you, our God!

6 Yet by grace we travel still,
gladly subject to your will;
by your truth, your perfect law,
love we are created for,
help us love you all the more.

77777 Tune by Elspeth Thompson

Scriptures: Exod 19–20, 33–34 Ps 69 Luke 12:50 Eph 2:13–17 Heb 12:18–29 Jas 1:25
Written: Herne Hill, SE London, 1–16 April 2016
In April 2016 my daily readings brought me to the central chapters of the Exodus, and further thought about the Law of God, the circumstances of its being given, and the Gospel of Christ which comes from the hand of the same loving and speaking God. My first draft was in 7777, but this seemed too compressed; the opening couplet also went through several changes and a different rhyme before reaching its final shape.

Deuteronomy 28:38–42
When the earth goes wrong

21   THE SEASONS, LORD, ARE IN YOUR HAND

1   The seasons, Lord, are in your hand;
and you have blessed our human race
with skills to measure, understand,
and track new worlds deep into space.

2   Yet how we foul what you made good!
the air we breathe, the fields we farm;
our rivers turn again to blood,
new plagues have come, new locusts
    swarm.

3   We grieve where forests once have
       grown,
the spreading desert, melting ice;
where little comes from what is sown
we lose all sense of paradise.

4   Have mercy on this earth, O Lord;
the changes we cannot control,
the healing we cannot afford,
the fractures we cannot make whole.

5   But show what difference we can make,
in travelling, trading with true care;
to learn to give before we take,
and spend in ways that all can share.

6   Lord Christ, the future leads to you;
'Your will be done', we learn to pray;
yours is the past, the present too;
give us the will to change today!

LM   Tune: MELCOMBE

Scriptures: Gen 1:28; 2:8,15; 3:17–19, 23; 8:22   Exod 7:14–24; 10:1–15   Deut 28:38–42   Joel 1:1–12
Haggai 1:5–6   Matt 6:10   Acts 20:35
Written: Herne Hill, SE London, 18–19 Nov 2015
Concern for conservation and a greener earth need never be the enemy of evangelism, an alternative to
it or a distraction from it. But even in places where it features in our prayers or our preaching, it seems to
surface rarely, if at all, in our songs. So here is another small text helping to narrow a large gap.

Ruth

The shortest book yet

22 IN THE DAYS OF DARKNESS LIGHT WILL ALWAYS SHINE

1 In the days of darkness
    light will always shine,
through a nation's crisis
    God provides a sign;
through this world's confusion
    some will love the truth:
in the years of judges—
    Naomi and Ruth!

2 Not for Hebrews only
    is the promised rest;
God has shown his mercy,
    foreigners are blessed.
Those who come for shelter
    under heaven's wings
look to God for guidance
    in the smallest things.

3 Bethlehem at harvest
    is the place to be;
after famine, plenty—
    fruit for all to see:
needy ones who seek him
    by God's hand are led,
widows find salvation
    in the House of Bread!

4 Kinsman and redeemer,
    lord sustaining life,
Ruth has found a husband,
    Boaz gains a wife;
in the line to David,
    she will take her place,
pattern of devotion,
    trophy of God's grace.

5 We who come long after
    stand where Ruth has stood;
every loss or setback
    God will work for good.
Jesus, Son of David,
    you have come for me;
from a land of shadows
    you have set me free.

6 Hallelujah! Saviour,
    in you we belong
firmly in your family,
    sing your harvest song.
Christ, you make us welcome
    through the hardest days;
Master, Friend and Bridegroom—
    yours be all the praise!

6565 Tune: RUTH

Scriptures: The Book of Ruth; also Judg 21:25   Matt 1:1–6, 2:1   Mark 2:18–20   Rom 1:1–4   Eph 5:25–27   Rev 21:2

Written: Bromley, Kent, 20-22 Oct 2011 (Bethlehem = 'Place of food', or 'House of bread'.)

On 30th October 2011 I was due to preach on Ruth at Hayes Lane Baptist Church, Bromley, in an 'over-view' series on Bible books, planned and mainly led by the minister David Hircock. I couldn't find a hymn which clearly reflected the whole book. The tune suddenly occurred to me as at night I was reading *Beyond All Words* by Alan Gaunt (2011), who also uses RUTH and calls it 'a favourite from childhood'—a senti-ment I echo. So, given the metre, I set to work in a week when even more people than usual asked 'Have you written any hymns lately?' and had a presentable draft ready by Oct 22. Our usual musician Jonathan Gooch (see p.9 and no.13 etc) was away that Sunday, but had pre-recorded the music for us; we sang it after the reading of and comments on ch.3. This was the first book in this Bible series which we could read complete and aloud (in its four natural parts) in one service.

Among friends over many years are notable Ruths—Butler, Cox, Day, Martin and Woodcraft.

Ruth 1:16–17

A daughter-in-law to her mother-in-law

23   BIBLE WORDS WE LOVE TO EXPLORE

1   Bible words we love to explore
    tell the plea of a daughter-in-law:
    'Don't ask me to leave you now –
    I won't turn back anyhow!
    Where you go, I shall go too;
    where you stay, I'll stay near you.

2   In your family I will join;
    your true God will now be mine.
    Where you die, there I will die;
    where you're buried, I shall lie.'
    That is the promise made by Ruth,
    knowing the Lord, his grace and truth.

77 77 77   Tune: TWINKLE TWINKLE, LITTLE STAR

Scriptures: Ruth 1:16–17
Written: Peckham, SE London, 2000, revised Bromley, Kent 21 Oct 2011.
See the notes to no.2; launched at Pilgrims' Way Primary School in the Old Kent Road, this song (needing a brief introduction!) was considerably revised for the service at Hayes Lane Baptist Church on Oct 30. One small sorrow was that on this occasion, most unusually, hardly any children were there to sing it.

2 Samuel 7:1–17

Disappointment

24   SOME THINGS WE LONG FOR

1 Some things we long for
   and long prepare for,
   and set our hearts on
   somehow, somewhere;
   then God corrects us
   and redirects us
   to what is better,
   yet hard to bear.

2 Some things we work for
   fervently hope for,
   looking ahead with
   our long-term plan;
   then the Lord shows us,
   because he knows us,
   that we must start back
   where we began.

3 Lord God, please deal with
   our disappointments,
   slowness to let go
   times that have gone.
   Your Spirit's filling
   shall make us willing
   to find and follow
   where you lead on.

4 Grant to your children
   your true perspective,
   always to love best
   what you command;
   seek first and foremost
   what you have promised,
   blessings unfailing
   from your wise hand.

5 Please come to change us,
   humble, renew us,
   making your pure will
   our heart's delight;
   let all our talking,
   thinking and walking,
   be for Christ Jesus
   good in your sight.

6 You gave a template
   for our ambitions
   in all the footsteps
   of your dear Son;
   so let us hear him,
   keep ever near him,
   pray in his pattern,
   your will be done.

Praise Trust   5554D   Tune: TUDDENHAM by Victor E Day

Scriptures: 2 Sam 7:1–17 1 Kgs 8:17–19 1 Chron 28:1–3 Isa 5:1–2 Jer 45:4–5 Matt 20:20–23; 21:18–20
Mark 5:18–20; 12:1–12 Luke 24:13–24 Acts 16:6–8 Gal 1:6–7 2 Tim 4:9–18
Written: Herne Hill, Feb 2015. Another of the suggested topics for new writing, on a list circulated by
the *Praise!* editorial group in Jan 2014. This also appealed to me, since it seemed a neglected theme com-
pared with the classic treatments of sin, forgiveness, redemption etc. Scripture has many examples of both
human disappointment and the rather different divine kind; this text has echoes of some of the Sunday
collects in The Book of Common Prayer (e.g. Easter 4, Trinity 6).

1 Kings 8:46

No-one who does not sin

25   BY NATURE WE ARE PRONE TO SIN

1   By nature we are prone to sin,
    from one true pathway swerving;
    in outward acts and shame within
    our death and hell deserving.
    But we have bowed before God's
        throne;
    in Christ we are forgiven,
    redeemed and called to be his own,
    and made the heirs of heaven.

2   Yet often, feeling wise or strong,
    some folly makes us stumble;
    how slow we are to own our wrong,
    unwilling to be humble!
    We find our failures hard to take,
    and hate to show our weakness,
    admit aloud the slips we make
    or turn to God in meekness.

3   So grant us, Saviour, here to know
    each fault, each limitation;
    in wisdom and in grace to grow,
    and grasp your great salvation.
    Our lapses whether great or small
    still need our true confessing:
    and for your love that heals them all;
    we owe all praise and blessing.

8787D iambic   Tune by Elspeth Thompson

Scriptures: 1 Kgs 8:46   1 Chron 6:36   Ps 51:1–12   Rom 3:23   Jas 5:16   1 John 1:8
Written: Herne Hill, SE London, 11–20 December 2016.
My original draft, prompted partly by an Advent sermon at Christ's Chapel in Dulwich, dealt with human vulnerability and self-deception. But I soon realised that these were two different subjects needing differ-ent hymns; the twin text in the same metre, dealing with the first subject, became 'In utter weakness we arrived' (no.44). With this one, Brian Edwards helped me to decide on the better of two possible opening lines.

   Some of us are almost proud (!) of our eloquence in bewailing the 'total depravity' of our natural, sinful state. But at the same time we can be sadly oblivious of the everyday annoyances which can test the patience of our friends, sometimes to breaking-point. Rudeness, lateness, impatience, interrupting, not listening, always needing the last word… It is hard to express such double standards in a hymn; but I have tried. Even if there were such things as trivial sins, we are not our own best judges! See also no.40.

1 Kings 18
Head count

26   WHEN NUMBERS ARE AGAINST US

1   When numbers are against us
and rival gods seem strong,
when truth appears defeated
by what is clearly wrong;
    the God of fire and water.
    of mountain, sea, and sky,
    the Lord God of Elijah
    will claim the victory!

2   When wars and earthquakes rumble
and fear or famine reign,
corruption stains whole nations
and earth travails in pain,
    when hearts and hands are failing,
    and every face grows pale,
    we turn afresh to Jesus
    whose words will never fail.

3   From Carmel to Mount Zion
the plan of God holds firm;
by grace we stand with prophets
and martyrs, through the storm:
    we join those first apostles
    to share the broken bread;
    we drink the cup of blessing,
    one body with one Head.

4   No tyrant or imposter
will have the final word;
the cross becomes our glory,
the gospel we have heard;
    if doubts or fears assail us,
    what will the future bring?
    our hope is in his promise –
    the advent of our King!

Praise Trust 7676D   Tune: EWING

Scriptures: 1 Kings 18   Luke 21:25ff:
Written: Bromley, Kent, 5 Dec 2010 (2nd Sunday in Advent) for Holy Trinity Church, Bromley Common, to reflect the appointed Scripture readings. The last line is the first of one version of John Chandler's 1837 translation of the Latin of Charles Coffin, 'Instantis adventum Dei'.

1 Chronicles 27:25–34

Work of all kinds, then and now

27   HARD-WORKING GOD, WHOSE GRACIOUS HAND

1   Hard-working God, whose gracious hand
sustains the life of every land,
the whole creation springs from you
and you make us creative too:
    you give your children all that's best
    of thought and feeling, work and rest;
as all things good are what you give,
so in your calling may we live.

2   Thank you for those who count our funds
and watch the way the market runs,
or oversee the treasuries
in cities, towns and villages.
    Thank you for those who farm the fields,
    and measure what each acre yields,
or train the climbing rows of vines
for choicest grapes and richest wines.

3   Thank you for those who tend the soil
where olives grow, for wood and oil,
for healing, nourishment and light,
whose lamps illuminate the night;

or lead their flocks across the hills,
    by expert care and breeding skills,
where camels sometimes swell the herd
and even donkeys hear God's word.

4   For leaders, called to serve their tribes
as counsellors, wise men and scribes,
who understand the use of words
and love the laws which are the Lord's:
    we thank you, God; for you alone
    give strength and wisdom to each one,
grant work for all in every place,
to serve our neighbours, by your grace.

5   We pray for those whose labour means
a sight today of rural scenes;
and those engulfed by towers of steel,
confined by screen, machine or wheel.
    For every trade to you is known;
    the image in us is your own:
your power creates, your grace restores;
in Christ our work, our world, are yours.

LMD   Tune: YE BANKS AND BRAES

Scriptures: based on 1 Chron 27:25–34

Written: 22–26 Nov 2011; revised May 2015 (v.1 added; others renumbered; the new 2 & 3 adjusted). The original version was written after planning and preaching a sermon on this chapter, reflecting some of the various jobs required for Solomon's kingdom. The late David Wright was one of those pleading for more hymns about work, while Mark Greene of The London Institute for Contemporary Christianity also requests more sermons (and prayers etc) on the subject. See also no.15 and the subject index.

Nehemiah 2:8

Building project

28   COME, LET US BUILD UP THE WALLS OF JERUSALEM

1 Come, let us build up the walls of
    Jerusalem
  where they are broken and
    blackened with flame;
  let us take heart and be strong
    with new energy,
  held and sustained by the
    power of God's name.

2 Christ's fellow-workers, we join this
    great company,
  stirred by his Spirit, compelled by
    his word,
  while we have time and
    today's opportunity,
  take our full share in the work
    of the Lord.

3 So grows the wall of each earthly
    Jerusalem,
  conquering setbacks,
    diversions, delays;
  ending disgrace, disappointment
    and ridicule,
  every advance shall resound
    to God's praise.

4 Sometimes most joyfully, often more
    doggedly,
  called to be faithful,
    obedient and true;
  Lord, make us work,
    as you work in us constantly,
  longing by grace to bring
    glory to you.

12 10 12 10   Tune: WAS LEBET, WAS SCHLEBET

Scriptures: Neh 2:17   1 Cor 3:10–13, 15:58   2 Cor 4:1, 6:1   Eph 5:15–16   Phil 2:12–13
Written: Bromley, Kent, and neighbourhood, Jan-July 2012
A hymn arising from my regular reading through this part of the Old Testament, when the text in the heading (including its natural rhythm) struck me with particular force, and led to some New Testament parallels and present-day applications. See also *Come, let us rebuild* by Bishop Anthony Poggo, 2013.

Nehemiah 8:10

Joy and strength

29   THE LORD IS THE SOURCE OF OUR LIFE

1 The Lord is the source of our life,
  his love has no limit or length;
  his mercy and truth will for ever
    endure,
  the joy of the Lord is our strength.
  Then strong in his joy, let us hear,
  respond to the power of his word
  to love one another in Christ,
  and live by the truth we have heard.

2 The way of the Lord is our path,
  the word of the Lord is our light;
  the hand of the Lord is upon us for
    good,
  to do what is pure in his sight.
  Then strong in his joy, let us walk
  the road which the pioneers trod,
  encourage each other in Christ,
  together to glorify God.

3 The church of the Lord is our home;
  and bought with the blood of his Son:
  the Lord is our Saviour, our strength and our
    song,
  our hope is the work he has done.
  Then strong in his joy, let us work
  and find how our burdens are shared,
  and serve one another in Christ,
  do all that his grace has prepared.

8 8 11 8 8888 anapaestic   Tune: JOY OF THE LORD by Jonathan Gooch (2010)

Scriptures: Ezra 3:11; 8:21–22   Neh 2:18; 8:9   Ps 117:2; 119:105   John 13:34   Acts 20:28
Gal 5:13; 6:2   Eph 2:10   1 Thess 4:18
Written: Bromley, Kent, Feb–May 2010

'The joy of the Lord is your strength' (Neh 8:10) is a text with a double resonance for me. While living in Bromley in 1960 I shared in a mission at St Luke's Deptford; the evangelist Guy Nicholson gave the student-team a daily 'motto' and this one stayed clearly in my mind.

Fifty years later, when I was back in Bromley after a 40-year absence, this was the annual motto at Hayes Lane Baptist Church, chosen and preached on by the pastor David Hircock. In February Jonathan Gooch suggested that I might try writing a hymn based on it; he would aim to compose the music.

After an early draft, in three 4-line stanzas, he said that it needed more of our response to what God in Christ has said and done. So I added the lines (5–8 of each verse) which act as a chorus-with-variations. My complete text reflects other Scriptures including themes from the context in Nehemiah—such as 'the hand of the Lord being upon them/us for good'. I first heard Johnny's tune on June 3rd, with two different versions of the 'chorus'. His friend and future wife Carol Ryan helped us to choose the first version which seemed easier to sing; Johnny did more work on the music and we introduced it on Sunday evening, 20th June.

Nehemiah 12:46

Words and music

30 IN PSALMS AND HYMNS OF JOYFUL PRAISE

1 In psalms and hymns of joyful praise,
   by songs in countless different ways,
   what riches we are given!
In text and tune, by words and deeds,
   in serving one another's needs,
   this earth is touched with heaven.

2 What fruit these passing years have seen!
What varied changes there have been
   to shake and shape God's church!
Yet Christ the Saviour does not change;
   his cross, his glory are not strange
   to those who truly search.

3 Who knows what future years may bring?
By grace our children's children sing;
   we join with them as one.
The promises of God shall stand,
   and all our times are in his hand
   through Christ, the eternal Son.

4 So let us, while it is today,
   lift heart and voice, give thanks and pray
   with every blended chord;
for every season, every year
is his, while one Great Day draws near,
   and ours, to serve the Lord.

886D   Tune: FIFTY YEARS by Roger Peach (2016)

Scriptures: Neh 12:46   Eph 5:19-20   Col 3:16   Heb 3:13; 13:8
Written: Herne Hill, SE London, 21–24 January 2016
Recorded: The Jubilate Big Sing, 'God of all human history', 2017.
The original version was written for the 50th anniversary celebration of *Youth Praise*; hence line 1: 'In Psalms and hymns of youthful praise'. Similar adjustments were made for more general use at 2.1 and 3.1, omitting references to 'fifty years'.

Job 38:7

The morning stars: God's music

31 THE GLORY OF THE MORNING

1 The glory of the morning was heralded in song,
with joyful stars for orchestras
while angels sang along.
The God of all creation, who gave the worlds their birth,
composed a tune for sun and moon
and music for the earth.

2 The glory of the midnight the shepherds run to see;
God speaks to them at Bethlehem:
your Saviour—this is he!
The God of our salvation sends heaven's choir to tell
in melody and harmony
of our Emmanuel.

3 The glory of the evening is in an upper room
where bread and wine become a sign
and Jesus leads the Psalm.
The God of our redemption the powers of earth condemn;
and silently he goes to die outside Jerusalem.

4 The glory of the ages lights up our darkest days;
in prison chain and brutal pain
believers pitch their praise.
The God of resurrection gives heart and voice to sing,
and still confess the faithfulness
of Christ the risen King.

5 The glory that is coming the trumpet will proclaim,
God's instrument, magnificent
to blazon Jesus' name.
The God of fresh creation, whose every word is true,
hears all our prayers and now prepares
a universe made new.

6 One Hallelujah chorus, one Spirit-given chord,
one symphony, one unity,
one everlasting Lord!
With every gift and talent we celebrate again
one special place, one God of grace,
one glory-filled Amen!

Tune: THE HOLLY AND THE IVY

Scriptures: Job 38:7   Matt 1:22–23; 24:30–31   Mark 14:12–26   Luke 2:1–16   Acts 16:22–25
1 Cor 15:52 Eph 6:20 Phil 1:12–14 1 Thess 4:16 Heb 11:32–40; 13:12 Rev 5:13–14; 11:15; 19:1; 21:1–5
Written: Bromley, Kent, 16-26 Nov 2008
Roger Bristow, Vicar of my parish church of Holy Trinity Bromley Common, asked for a carol to be sung at the 2008 Carol Service. I took this to mean a new one, so this was my second attempt to ride on the popular familiarity of 'The holly and the ivy' (see also 'Two thousand years of sorrow', no.41 in *Walking by the River*, 2008).

The Psalms (one)
Singing to the Lord (1)

32 EARTH'S CELEBRATION OF GOD'S WAYS

1 Earth's celebration of God's ways
   is heard at best imperfectly;
   but all our major, minor praise
   on high or ordinary days
   still echoes heaven's harmony.

2 When wounds are fresh or scars remain
   our songs emerge reluctantly;
   yet saints who face extremes of pain,
   the knife, the gun, the fire, the chain,
   praise their dear Lord most joyously.

3 When grief has made our spirits numb
   the trusting heart sings silently;
   when melodies are rendered dumb
   faith still perceives God's kingdom come
   by love's unconquered victory.

4 Then finding gain in bitter loss,
   each hour, each anniversary,
   we have a Friend who sings with us,
   and psalms still treasured at his cross
   shall rise with Easter energy.

5 And comes that day that rights all wrongs,
   the new creation's infancy,
   then perfect praise unites all tongues
   in words and music, hymns and songs
   from one redeemed community.

Praise Trust   88 888   Tune: RUMSEY by Sophie Killingley (2013)

Scriptures: Zeph 3:17   Mark 15:34   Luke 23:46   Acts 16:25   Heb 2:12   Jas 1:2   1 Peter 4:12–14
Written: Bromley, Kent, 2010
First published: *Evangelicals Now* (monthly), Jan 2016
To mark the 75th Anniversary of the Hymn Society of Great Britain and Ireland (to which I had belonged for about a third of its life) several writers were invited to submit a new hymn text on the theme of praise and thanksgiving. This was mine, now slightly adjusted; the chosen hymn, which I was glad to introduce at our Belfast celebration in Sept 2011, was Janet Wootton's 'When Miriam's daughters rise and sing'. The music for that hymn, selected from among many entries, was John Barnard's CHERRY HINTON.

The Psalms (two)
Singing to the Lord (2)

33   HOW CAN WE FIND THE WORDS TO SING

1   How can we find the words to sing
how massive is God's favour,
who shows such mercy to our world
by sending such a Saviour?

2   We'll turn again to David's psalms
whose grief and joy still reach us;
we sing the songs of yesterday
and let the prophets teach us.

3   We'll look ahead to what's in store
by God's own promise given;
we'll sing tomorrow's songs today
and join the praise of heaven.

4   And while this present moment lasts
for gospel proclamation,
we'll sing new songs that bring today
good news of our salvation.

5   For Christ who died for us, now lives;
the Lord who changes never:
so let us love him, keep his word,
and sing his praise for ever.

8787 iambic   Tune: ST COLUMBA

Scriptures: Ps 104:33   John 14:15   Eph 5:19   Col 3:16   Heb 13:8   1 John 4:14
Written: Herne Hill, SE London, June–July 2016.
This text grew from a single line which stayed single for some time; one of the resulting stanzas took a great deal of re-writing. Readers are invited to guess which line, and which stanza.

Psalm 25: 4–12

Teach us your way

34 TEACH US, OUR GOD, THE WAY OF GOODNESS

1 Teach us, our God, the way of goodness,
show us your paths of righteousness;
so may we never take diversions
but walk where you are sure to bless.

2 Teach us, our God, the way of wisdom,
knowing the truth that makes us free;
not taken in by smart delusions,
but find in Christ our liberty.

3 Teach us, our God, the way of justice,
not flinching from the hardest choice;
and where our silence would be shameful,
grant us the strength to raise our voice.

4 Teach us, our God, the way of mercy,
Christ died for us, and Christ arose;
surely we shall forgive our neighbours,
our brothers, sisters, friends and foes.

5 Teach us, our God, the way of service,
the pain and joy of sacrifice;
not holding back one mite, one moment,
since we were bought at such a price.

6 Teach us, our God, the way of courage,
when every step seems full of tears,
face every conflict with your weapons
and by your Spirit end our fears.

7 Teach us, our God, the way of glory,
to set our hearts on things above;
then confidently greet the future,
the kingdom of your perfect love.

9898 Tune: SPIRITUS VITAE

Scriptures: Ps 23:3; 25:4–12   Matt 6:3   Mark 10:42–45   John 8:32   Acts 10:39–43   1 Cor 6:20; 7:23
Gal 5:1   Eph 4:32; 6:10   Col 3:1–4
Written: Streatham & Herne Hill, SW & SE London, 9–10 Oct 2016
Uniquely for me, the idea (and familiar tune!) for this text came in a half-remembered dream, some of
which I tried to recapture and clarify over the next day or two.

Psalm 90:10

Growing older

35   OUR VIEW ACROSS THE MILES GONE BY

1   Our view across the miles gone by
  is filled with thankfulness.
 The years that crept now seem to fly;
 past peaks and valleys, low and high,
  our Lord and God we bless
  his goodness we confess.

2   Some paths are cloudy, some are clear,
  as we look fondly back;
 the changing focus year by year,
 regret or comfort, hope or fear,
  yet nothing can we lack
  while keeping on his track.

3   We cannot know the where or when
  of landmarks on the hill;
 the measured threescore years and ten
 may pass, but will not come again,
  for time does not stand still,
  but runs, for good or ill.

4   And though we march, and love to sing,
  the future none can tell;
 we know not what a day may bring,
 but learn to trust the sovereign King
  of heaven and earth and hell;
  our God does all things well.

5   So, Christian, while it is today
  be ready for his call;
 while travelling on the homeward way
 look to the cross, and boldly say,
  while worlds and empires fall,
  Christ is my All-in-all.

Praise Trust   86 8866   REPTON; or new tune needed

Scriptures: Gen 47:9–10   Lev 19:32   Josh 14:10–13; 23:14   1 Sam 7:12   Ps 90:10   Isa 55:6
Luke 2:25–38   1 Tim 5:9–10   2 Tim 4:6–8   Tit 2:1–5   Jas 4:14
Written: Herne Hill, SE London, February 2014
One of the topics suggested for new writing in early 2014, as proposed by the *Praise!* editorial group, was 'Growing older'. Being in that bracket myself I could hardly decline the invitation. Depending on where we draw the boundaries of ageing, there are many elderly heroes and heroines in Scripture, and much instruction and counsel—far too many and too much to include all of them among these references.

Psalm 107: 23–32 (one)

The sea is his, and he made it (1)

36   WATERS, OCEANS AND SEAS

1   Waters, oceans and seas;
every wave and deep-running tide,
every pool, every bay,
is the care of its Maker and Guide.

2   Coasts and islands of peace and prayer,
delight in colour and calm.
Storm and tempest bring death and danger,
deep waters warning of harm.

3   Routes and roads to be found,
travelled pathways mapped and explored;
bring good trade, bring good news,
face to face with the works of the Lord.

4   Soon the King who once calmed the waters
returns as judge of the earth:

5   Then shall all be redeemed,
by the Lord of land, air and sea;
what was lost is restored,
what was bound is for ever set free.

Irregular   Tune: SAILING BY, by Ronald Binge (1963)

Scriptures: Gen 1: 9–10   1 Kgs 9:26–28; 10:22   Ps 95:5; 98:7–9; 107:23–32   Ezek 27   Jonah 1   Matt
16:27; 19:28   Mark 6:35–41   Acts 16:11–12; 27   Rom 8:20–21   2 Cor 1:25
Written: Herne Hill, SE London, 15–17 Nov 2015
Here is an example of the tune coming first; the familiar late-night lead-in to the *Shipping Forecast* on BBC
Radio 4. The idea for the words was prompted by two magazine articles. One pointed out that while many
saw the sea as a barrier between nations, to others it was a highway of communication. The second dwelt
on the extraordinary quantity and variety of unexplored life in the ocean depths. A first draft included
both these concepts, but as it proved too long I divided it into two separate texts, both for this music: see
no.37 following.

Psalm 107: 23–32 (two)
The sea is his, and he made it (2)

37   SEAS WHERE CREATURES ABOUND

1   Seas where creatures abound
far beyond our wisdom to name;
in the depths, in the dark,
are great wonders which no-one can
tame.

2   But when nations take pride in power,
wage wars destructive of life,
seas are cauldrons of fear and struggle
and vast new waters of strife.

3   Yet we still see on earth
some sublime reflections of heaven;
by God's grace he sustains
what to all generations is given.

4   So the promise shall stand for ever,
the word of God cannot fail:

5   Soon all things are made new,
where the seas no longer destroy;
no more pain, no more death,
in the kingdom of Christ and of joy.

Irregular   Tune: SAILING BY, by Ronald Binge (1963)

Scriptures: Gen 1: 9–10   Ps 95:5; 104:24–26; 107:23–32   Ezek 27   Rom 8:20–21   Rev 21:1–5
Written: Herne Hill, SE London, 15–17 Nov 2015
See the notes to No.36, 'Waters, oceans and seas'. And 'our oceans are in crisis… they are source of all life, covering nearly three-quarters of the earth's surface and home to millions of species—their importance cannot be over-stated… they are the life-blood of our planet': Tom Bawden, 2017.

Psalm 119:73

Creation and revelation

38   YOU HAVE KNOWN ME BEFORE MY BIRTH

1 You have known me before my birth
and designed me in every part;
for the path of my life on earth
you have planned from the very start.

2 You have led me to hear your call,
and you gave me a heart to pray:
what I need, you provide it all;
you have brought me to walk your way.

3 You prepare every day and night,
and provide me with loving friends;
giving freedom to choose the right
in a friendship that never ends.

4 You have taught me to love your word,
every promise and each command;
and my cries you have always heard,
for you hold me in your right hand.

5 And your mercy will lift me up,
and forgive me when I go wrong;
when in trouble you are my hope,
in my weakness you make me strong.

6 By the love that the Father gives,
by the Spirit who works in me;
by the Saviour who died, yet lives,
I shall be what I'm meant to be.

8888 (distinctive)   Tune by Elspeth Thompson

Scriptures: Ps 119:73; 139:13–16   Prov 17:17; 18:24; 27:10   Jer 1:4–5   2 Cor 12:10   Phil 4:19   Heb 13:20–21
Written: Herne Hill, SE London, 25–27 June 2016
While reading Psalm 119 in my daily prayer time, I was struck by verse 73: 'Your hands made me and formed me: give me understanding to learn your commands'. Here in a nutshell is the truth of creation and revelation; God made me—us—and also made us capable of learning his commands with a view to trust and obedience.

Psalm 126

The harvest of God's word

39 WHEN THE LORD RESTORED HIS PEOPLE

1 When the LORD restored his people
it seemed just like a dream;
our mouths were filled with laughter
and gladness reigned supreme.
They said among the nations,
'The LORD has done great things';
for all that he has done for us
a thankful people sings.

2 LORD, we pray, restore our fortunes
like streams that once were dry;
then those who sow in sorrow
will reap with shouts of joy:
and those who go out weeping,
with good seed to be sown,
will come back with a harvest
singing praise to God alone.

3 Glory, glory to the Father,
and praises to the Son,
all honour to the Spirit,
our God, the Three-in-One!
For Jesus is the Sower,
the seed, his precious word;
and God will bless, wherever
his Good News is truly heard.

8676 7686   Tune: THE YELLOW ROSE OF TEXAS

Based on: Ps 126
Other Scriptures: Job 8:21   Ps 85:1   Isa 35:10; 55:10–12   Luke 8:4–15
Written: Kendal, Cumbria, 29 July 2012
While staying with David and Helen Hannant in Kendal, our conversation turned, for totally different reasons, to Psalm 126 and to the tune suggested here. In a moment of discovery I realised that the two might just fit together.

Psalm 139:23–24

The Searcher of hearts and the sins of the saints

40   SEARCH OUR HEARTS, WE PRAY, LORD

1 Search our hearts, we pray, Lord;
shine your light within,
when we call our failings
anything but sin:

2 Proud of our achievements,
though our aims are wrong;
you can see our motives,
tainted all along.

3 Search our lame excuses
where we shift the blame,
seeing faults in others
while we do the same.

4 You, O Christ, can cleanse us,
judge us and forgive:
in the light you give us
let us walk, and live.

Praise Trust   6565   Tune: CASWALL or NORTH COATES

Scriptures: Ps 19:12–14; 51:6; 139:23–24   Jer 17:9   Matt 7:3–5   John 2:24–25   Rom 2:21–23; 12:3   Heb 4:12-13   1 John 1:8

Written: Herne Hill, SE London, 6–7 March 2016

It is easy for preachers to fasten on the obvious sins of unbelievers while ignoring (or hardly being aware of) sins within the church or in ourselves: self-importance, laziness, envy, belittling others, complaining, half-truths, love of power, showing off, failure to listen, keeping people waiting, etc. This was written with those situations in mind—but thinking of past rather than current experiences; see also no.25. For this text, I was persuaded by TAG to reduce its six stanzas to four by dropping my original 4 and 6.

Proverbs 17:6

Grandchildren and grandparents

41   WHAT JOY IT IS TO SEE OUR CHILDREN'S CHILDREN

1   What joy it is to see our children's children!
The growing family of our closest kin;
each birth, each boy or girl, each man or woman,
alike yet different, full of rich potential,
with minds to open and with hearts to win
as God's amazing miracles begin.

2   How good it is to know our children's children!
To work and play with them, to laugh or cry,
to talk and listen, teach and learn together,
to share the word of God and its surprises,
enjoy the questions who and where and why,
and find the treasures money cannot buy.

3   How great it is to love our children's children!
To pray, give thanks, and with them sing God's praise,
to know today, whatever comes tomorrow,
delight or pain, reversal or achievement,
you, Lord, keep watch in love on all our ways,
the Source and Guide and Goal of all our days.

11 10 11 11 10 10   new tune needed

Scriptures: Gen 45:8–11   Deut 4:9   Ruth 4:13–22   Psa 78:5–7; 103:17–18; 128:5–6   Prov 17:6   Ezek 37:24–28   Rom 11:38   2 Tim 1:5

Written: Herne Hill, SE London, Feb 2014

When 'Grandchildren' was among the themes for new hymns, suggested by the *Praise!* editorial group in Jan 2014, it seemed a natural choice for me as a grateful Grandpa to attempt something. My parents saw all six of their children's children; Marjorie my wife knew four of ours, while I have had the joy of knowing twelve. This was written in February, soon after the first approach; I remain unsure about the likely occasions for its use.

Proverbs 17:17

Friends

42   I'M THANKING GOD FOR SO MANY PEOPLE

1 I'm thanking God for so many people,
   people who know me and still love me;
   thank you, Lord, for all these people,
   people who love you too.
   Yes, I give thanks for so many people,
   people who come and people who call me;
   thank you, Lord, for all these people,
   people who call to you.

2 I'm thanking God for so many people,
   people who sit or stand beside me;
   thank you, Lord, for all these people,
   people still with me too.
   Yes, I give thanks for so many people,
   people who talk and people who listen;
   thank you, Lord, for all these people,
   people who talk with you.

3 I'm thanking God for so many people,
   people who help and people who teach me;
   thank you, Lord, for all these people,
   people who learn things too.
   Yes, I give thanks for so many people,
   people who give their time and trouble;
   thank you, Lord, for all these people,
   people with time for you.

4 I'm thanking God for so many people,
   people who hurt me, people who pain me;
   thank you, Lord, for all these people,
   people whom I hurt too.
   Yes, I give thanks for so many people,
   people who love me and forgive me;
   thank you, Lord, for all these people,
   people forgiven by you.

5 I'm thanking God for so many people,
   people who may not often see me;
   thank you, Lord, for all these people,
   people all known to you.
   Yes, I give thanks for so many people,
   people with gifts beyond all counting;
   people with love that I can't measure,
   people beloved by you.

Irregular   new tune needed, in folk/spiritual style

Scriptures: Prov 17:17; 18:24; 27:10,17   John 15:12-17
Written: Herne Hill, SE London, August 17-30, 2015
This grew from work on a now discarded text, 'I'm thinking of so many people'; thinking moved into thanking.

Ecclesiastes 3:11

Many things

43   GOD OF ALL BEING, BEAUTY, FORM

1 God of all being, beauty, form,
of number, weight and measure,
you give us nature, seed and life,
our true, eternal treasure:
you made the rocks and sands and skies,
our fire and precious metals,
all beasts and cattle, fish and fowl,
great trees and fragile petals.

2 Your image shaped our human form,
a hint of unseen glories;
and when your Son was seen on earth
we marvelled at his stories;
for here is so much pain and wrong,
such emptiness, such sadness,
in flood and flame, in war and waste;
how can we sing with gladness?

3 Great God, we share the human blame
for much of mortal sorrow;
we cannot grasp the 'why' and 'how'
nor look beyond tomorrow.
We wrestle with the mysteries
and long to find their meaning;
yet do not know ourselves, or see
the end from the beginning.

4 Our Father, you have sent your Son
enduring, suffering, giving;
to be our life, our strength and song,
the spring of all our living.
As you still face the worst with us
when every hope unravels,
so may your perfect will be done
through all our earthly travels.

8787D iambic   Tune: GOLDEN SHEAVES, or new tune

Scriptures: Gen 1–2   Eccles 3:11   Isa 46:8–10   Matt 6:10   John 16:33   Rom 8:18–23
Jas 4:14   1 John 4:14–16
Written: Herne Hill, SE London, 2013–15
That is, summer to winter 2013 and July 2015. I cannot now recall what prompted these lines.

Ecclesiastes 5:15

Nothing in, nothing out

44   IN UTTER WEAKNESS WE ARRIVED

1   In utter weakness we arrived,
dependent, helpless, fragile;
and struggled long before we lived
and moved, upright and agile.
So came our God in human form,
an infant in a manger;
while others kept him clean and warm,
and fed, and safe from danger.

2   And as our brains and bodies grew
we found ourselves more able,
while daily learning something new,
and seeming firm and stable.
But still we had to understand
how much we need each other;
so Christ was strengthened by the hand
of sister, friend and brother.

3   But then in pain and nakedness
he hung outside the city,
and from the cross he spoke to bless
and save, in love and pity.
In weakness, too, we come to die,
on other arms dependent;
but then in Christ to reign on high,
in his pure robes resplendent.

8787D iambic   Tune: ERMUNTRE DICH, or new tune needed

Scriptures: Job 1:21   Eccles 5:15   Matt 2:13–15   Luke 2:6–7; 8:1–3 ; 23:33–34; 39–43
John 19:38–42   1 Tim 6:7   2 Tim 2:12   Rev 7:9–10
Written: Herne Hill; SE London, December 2016
Part of the origin of this hymn is explained in the notes to 'By nature we are prone to sin' (no.25). It also owes much to an address at the 2015 Evangelical Ministry Assembly (EMA) in London. Professor John Wyatt showed there that God's plan is for us to be totally dependent on others at both ends of our life on earth—as it was for his Son Jesus Christ. This gives a clear perspective to the needs of both newborn and dying people, their families and carers.

Ecclesiastes 12:9–11
Many books

45   THEY WRITE WHAT MANY READ

1   They write what many read
in every age;
Lord, show us what we truly need
from page to page.

2   They weave each patterned word
with confidence;
we read what they have seen and heard
with sharpened sense

3   Sometimes the news is good,
the story clear,
the message quickly understood
for all to hear.

4   But often in their theme
are sombre things;
the wrong we do or speak or dream,
that wounds and stings.

5   Or parables and signs,
in verse or prose,
with half-concealed or coded lines
of joys or woes.

6   We value light and dark,
the skills they use;
but mortals only make their mark
as God shall choose.

7   Grant, Lord, that as by grace
their voice lives on,
your truth shall stand, and keep its place
when they are gone.

6484   new tune needed

Scriptures: Ps 45:1   Eccles 12:9–11   Zech 1:5–6   2 John 12   3 John 13
Written: Herne Hill, SE London, May–June 2016
These verses began life in a 6464 metre but grew into 6484, which I have not found elsewhere. My original first line, lying dormant with a few scribbles for a while, was 'They weave a web of words', which partly survives in verse 2. The 'new' opening phrase, from an early 20th-century prayer, has stayed with me since boyhood, and is used by others in both verse and prose. There do not seem to be many hymns specifically about writing and writers, yet for many people this is still a regular occupation, where we either value or take for granted the work of others. The supreme example is the Bible, but hymns are not excluded.

Isaiah 48:18
True grace, real peace

46   PEACE WILL FLOW OUT LIKE A RIVER

1   Peace will flow out like a river
when we heed the Lord's commands:
justice like the mighty ocean;
earth and sky are in his hands.

2   God gives peace to all his people,
all who tremble at his word;
rescue reaches every nation
where his voice is truly heard.

3   Grace is like a living fountain,
peace a true life-giving stream;
Jesus shows how much he treasures
those he suffered to redeem.

4   Lord, your grace and peace shall bless us
by your holy Spirit's power;
yours the costly love that saves us
in our worst or weakest hour.

5   Yours the glory, Hallelujah!
Songs enrich our earthly days;
soon in your renewed creation
grace and peace shall fill our praise.

Praise Trust   Tune: PEACE IS FLOWING LIKE A RIVER

Scriptures: Isa 48:18; 66:12   John 14:27   Rom 1:7   1 Cor 1:3   2 Cor 1:2   Rev 21:1–5
Written: Herne Hill, SE London, 3–7 March 2016
Having been invited (again) to sing the popular all-purpose song 'Peace is flowing like a river', I thought (again) that the basic texts in Isaiah needed a song which reflected the context, making it clear that such peace is God's gift, that it is conditional, and that it is preceded by God's grace; only so can the captives be set free. The danger of songs that set out to say everything is that they end up saying little or nothing.

Isaiah 55

Foretaste of the gospel

47   ALL WHO ARE THIRSTY, COME

1 All who are thirsty, come!
The feast of life is free;
come eat and drink, you hungry ones,
no price, no entry fee!
Why waste your wealth on things
that will not satisfy,
or spend your strength for this world's goods
instead of God Most High.

2 Listen, that you may live:
God's covenant is sure:
his sovereign purpose will prevail,
his promises endure.
All peoples of the earth,
all nations, hear his voice;
draw near to worship, prove to be
the people of his choice.

3 Seek God with all your heart,
and while he may be found;
abandon rebel thoughts and ways
and see his grace abound.
God's ways are not as ours;
as high as heaven from earth,
but work his everlasting plan
and bring to us new birth.

4 Words coming from his mouth
shall not return in vain,
but like the rain that blesses us
bring life and fruit again:
this is for God's own praise
and will not be destroyed;
instead of thorns shall blossoms spring
by all the earth enjoyed.

5 Let us go out in joy
and be led forth in peace,
to join with trees and flowers and hills
in songs that never cease.
For we have been redeemed
from all that could enslave;
to Christ the Lord be praise and love;
whose name alone can save.

SMD   Tune: DIADEMATA

Based on: Isaiah 55

Other Scriptures: 1 Chron 16:33   Ps 96:12   Isa 35:10   John 4:10–14; 7:37   Rev 22:17

Written: Herne Hill, SE London, Oct–Nov 2016

Prompted by a reading of this chapter at Evensong in Oxford (30th Oct), and making a new start from the first line of a discarded text written more than thirty years earlier.

Jonah 3:1–2

A second time

48   GOD WHO GIVES THE SECOND CHANCE

1   God who gives the second chance,
calling, calling more than once:
patriarchs, apostles, kings,
priests and prophets knew these things:
how our patient Lord is kind,
guiding us to seek and find.

2   Abraham and Jacob found
how God's grace and love abound;
Jonah, Peter, Thomas, James,
Mark, and countless other names:
how God's patience dealt with them,
slow to punish or condemn.

3   All our years are but a breath;
soon will come the dust of death:
who knows what a day may spell;
peace or torment, heaven or hell?
All God's gifts are ours to take
while we live, and keep awake.

4   God still gives the second chance
in new scenes, new circumstance;
let us not presume on this,
never more his call dismiss,
not demanding why or how:
Christ is near; his time is now!

Praise Trust   77 77 77   Tune: ENGLAND'S LANE

Scriptures: Gen 21:1–5; 32:22–30   Jonah 3:1–2   John 20:24–29; 21:15–19   2 Cor 6:1–2   2 Tim 4:11
Jas 4:14   2 Pet 3:9
Written: Herne Hill, SE London, 14-15 Feb 2016

Jonah is the most obvious example of someone who was given a second chance by God. But there are many other examples in the Bible, some of which are touched on or hinted at in this hymn and the Scripture references. There are also countless examples of second, third and subsequent 'chances' outside and since Bible times; but also warnings that they are only for this life, and do not last indefinitely. The immediate prompting for this hymn came from a sermon on Jonah chapter 3, preached by Anthony Buckley, Chaplain of Alleyn's School, at Christ's Chapel, Dulwich, in February 2016.

The New Testament
Travelling with the Scriptures

49 THE CLEAR VOICE OF GOD IS CALLING US BY NAME

1 The clear voice of God is calling us by name,
   to journeys for which we are set apart;
   the New Testament will light the inner flame
   for travels with the gospel in our heart.
       So to Bethlehem and Nazareth and Galilee we'll go,
       on roads which Jesus Christ has made his own;
       to the city of Jerusalem—there our Guide will show,
       the mountain where salvation is made known.

2 Those far places will become well-trodden ground,
   as Scripture lights the path and feeds the soul;
   with our hearts warmed and our minds made clear and sound.
   we're walking with the Lord who makes us whole.
       To Damascus and to Antioch and Cyprus we will go,
       and look—the planted seeds are taking root;
       and in Troas and in Philippi we shall surely know
       how lives that God has touched are bearing fruit.

3 Sometimes we shall meet with trouble on our way,
   and persecution, martyrdom or pain;
   the Lord Christ is our companion every day,
   and when we fall, he lifts us up again.
       So to Athens and to Corinth and to Ephesus we move,
       to Crete and Malta, Rhegium and Rome,
       with our feet upon the thoroughfare, eyes are fixed above,
       as citizens of heaven and of home.

11 10 11 10 15 10 14 10   Tune: THE ROAD TO THE ISLES

Scriptures: The sixteen place-names can be traced in a concordance; other Scriptures include: Ps 119:105
Isa 43:1   Luke 8:11, 15; 24:32   John 10:3   Acts 14:22   Phil 3:20; Col 3:1   2 Tim 1:7
Written: Herne Hill, SE London, 26–28 March (Easter) 2016
The Scottish 'Road to the Isles' runs from Fort William to Mallaig, with 'the far Coolins' (the Cuillin
Mountains on the Isle of Skye) as a distant goal. In the 1940s my mother used to play and sing this march-
ing song of a hundred years ago; in 1982 our family of six travelled some of the route, celebrated in the
lyrics by evoking many of the places on the way. This text adopts the tune and the idea for a different
journey, travelled literally by many but available spiritually to all. Earlier drafts of this text were in the
singular, with fewer rhymes.

The four Gospels—one
What Jesus said (1)

50   HE SAID, THE SPIRIT OF THE LORD

1 He said, the Spirit of the Lord
is with me, to proclaim
hope for the poor, the prophet's word
of freedom in God's name.

2 He said, blind eyes receive their sight,
and silent tongues can talk;
instead of death come life and light
where helpless feet now walk.

3 He said to winds and waves 'Be still!'
and told the storm to cease;
so for our fears and storms, he will
bring healing, calm and peace.

4 He said the meek ones can be strong
while pleading on their knees,
to pray for those who do us wrong
and love our enemies.

5 He said, 'My peace I leave with you';
displayed his hands and side:
the marks of him whose word is true,
the living one who died.

6 Christ Jesus, risen from the dead,
gives us his Spirit's power,
to show what he has done and said
until God's final hour.

Praise Trust   CM   Tune: ST FULBERT, ST MAGNUS, or brisk new tune

Scriptures: Luke 4:14–19, and selections from all the Gospels
Written: Herne Hill, SE London, October 2015
There still seems to be a dearth of hymns quoting the teaching of Jesus. Here are two (originally a series of four, with 8 stanzas each) incorporating some of the things he said, mostly in summary form, so quotation-marks are kept to a minimum; see no.51.

The four Gospels—two

What Jesus said (2)

51 HE SAID HE CAME TO SEEK THE LOST

1 He said he came to seek the lost,
  to find us and to save;
  he warned us of the coming cost
  but looked beyond the grave.

2 He said he came to work, to serve,
  not to be served by us;
  that we must learn from his great love,
  for he must face the cross.

3 He said, I am the life, the way,
  the truth, the living bread;
  the vine, the resurrection day,
  the firstborn from the dead.

4 He said he would be crucified;
  betrayed by one false friend:
  he shouted 'Finished!' as he died;
  but that was not the end.

5 For as he said, he rose again
  in triumph from the tomb,
  to see the fruit of all his pain;
  rejoice—the King has come!

6 Our Father, may we heed his words
  and trust what he has done;
  Christ Jesus, Teacher, Saviour, Lord,
  and your beloved Son.

Praise Trust CM tune: ST FULBERT, ST MAGNUS, or brisk new tune

Scriptures: Luke 19:10, and selections from all the Gospels
Written: Herne Hill, SE London, October 2015
See the notes to no.50

Matthew 1:18–25

Emmanuel: God with us (1)

52   AS CHRISTMAS STARTS WITH CHRIST

1 As Christmas starts with Christ
and bells ring out his birth,
so he provides the feast
and blesses all the earth:
    Good gifts to bring,
    good food to share,
    good songs to sing,
    good news to hear!

2 Bright stars and trees will shine
along the busy street;
each one a tiny sign
of God's own Christmas treat:
    The birthday of
    Emmanuel,
    whose total love
    no words can tell.

3 And all the world still needs
to find what Christ can do—
his saving words and deeds
makes things and people new.
    As Christmas starts,
    the Christ arrives,
    who knows our hearts
    and rules our lives.

6666.4444   Tune: WEST WORTHING by John Barnard (2009)

Scriptures: Isa 55:1–2   Matt 1:18–25   Luke 2:10–11   John 2:24–25   2 Cor 5:17, 9:15   Rev 21:5
Written: Bromley, Kent, 11-18 October 2009
A response to an invitation to write a carol matching the 'Christmas starts with Christ' campaign launched by 'ChurchAds.Net' as 'The Christmas Factor Competition'. John Barnard composed a tune at short notice, and after delays due to days away and the need to submit electronically, it was sent with only minutes to spare for the November deadline. After which, we heard no more.

Matthew 1:21–23

Emmanuel: God with us (2)

53   ENCOUNTER WITH EMMANUEL

1 Encounter with Emmanuel—
   or is it just with Christmas?
   The lights, the toys, the jingle bell,
   the food and drink and gifts as well–
   or One of whom the Scriptures tell
   that he has come to save us?

2 Encounter with Emmanuel:
   the friends who gather round him
   are moved to ask 'Who then is this,
   who lifts the weight of our distress,
   who does not blame but loves to bless?'
   Praise God—in Christ we find him!

3 Encounter with Emmanuel,
   with two or three or thousands;
   we see him heal, we hear him teach,
   he gives his time for all, for each,
   then sends us to the world to preach
   Good News for all who trust him.

4 Encounter with Emmanuel,
   is this the King from heaven?
   He said he would be lifted high;
   was this to show how he would die?
   At Christmas we can testify
   Our Saviour lives for ever!

87 8887 Tune: ENCOUNTER by Jonathan Gooch (2011)

Scriptures: Matt 1:21-23; 10:1–10   Mark 4:41   John 12:32–33

Written: , Bromley, Kent, 6 Nov 2011

Yes, another Christmas invitation, this time from Steve Piggott, Pastor of Rehoboth Grace Baptist Chapel in Horsham, W Sussex. In April 2011 he conducted the wedding of Jonathan Gooch and Carol Ryan, at Wattisham, Suffolk; subsequently he asked if Johnny and I could offer a new Christmas song for the December 5th concert in Horsham. I gave Johnny some texts, but then wrote this when Steve defined his theme more closely as 'Encounter(s) with Emmanuel'. Johnny's music seemed more suitable for a solo, and with his help the text was finalised less than 24 hours before the concert.

Matthew 2:13–23 (one)
Egypt, slavery and sanctuary (1)

54 THE LAND OF PYRAMIDS AND PALMS

1 The land of pyramids and palms
  was known for craft and cruelty;
  and named in stories, laws and psalms
  by tribes redeemed from slavery.

2 For Egypt's kings were harsh and crude,
  and many deeds of evil done;
  but freedom came from shedding blood:
  the paschal lamb, or firstborn son.

3 New Egypts, Babylons and Romes
  oppress God's people, crushing them;
  till from the Father's glory comes
  his promised Christ, in Bethlehem.

4 But in that long-awaited dawn
  see Herod's men with sharpened knives;
  one couple, with one newly-born,
  escape to Egypt with their lives.

5 And many strangers since that year,
  asylum-seekers, refugees,
  still look for sanctuary and care
  from those who welcome such as these.

6 How many Josephs, travelling light,
  have thanked their God for help like this?
  What Marys praised him, in their flight,
  that all the power on earth is his?

7 Yet in this world we never know
  what millions more are turned away,
  with none to love, no place to go,
  no roof by night nor food by day.

8 God help us feel and understand
  where people suffer, why and how;
  that we in Christ, heart, voice and hand
  may love and serve our neighbours, now.

LM   Tune: WINCHESTER NEW

Scriptures: Exod 1–2; 12–14; 20:1–3   Deut 23:7   Ps 114; 78:12–13; 136:10–15   Matt 2:1, 13–23; 22:34–40   Heb 13:1–3   Rev 11:8; 18

Written: Herne Hill, SE London, 6–8 November 2015

A poem, maybe a potential song lyric or even (given the right tune) a hymn? A headline about travel problems in Egypt, for Britons among others (6th Nov 2015), reminded me that this ancient and gifted nation has a generally negative role in Scripture, whether in narrative (Exodus), song (the Psalms), or symbolism (Rev 11). It is the land of cruel slavery, the 'house of bondage' (AV) from which God's people Israel needed to be redeemed. This is reflected in spirituals such as 'Go down, Moses' and a handful of hymns, mainly Psalm paraphrases such as my own versions of 78, 80, 81, 114, 135. But the 'flight into Egypt' by Joseph, Mary and their holy Child does not seem to feature much in hymns or even carols; some of the best-known stop short of actually naming the land of their temporary sanctuary. This was my attempt to fill a gap, written on that 'headline' day and the next. It was the first hymn of mine to be put together at the computer keyboard rather than first in a draft form with pen and paper. It may seem impertinent to write thus of a country I have never visited, but Scripture gives us much to go on. And some two centuries ago Bishop Heber waxed eloquent about Greenland, Ceylon (Sri Lanka) and 'Afric'; even India, before he ever got there. My nearest claim: Israel, Jordan, and eldest and youngest sons who travelled in Egypt more than once. The latter graduated in Egyptology, studying at Liverpool under Prof Kenneth Kitchen and Dr Alan Millard.

Matthew 2: 13–23 (two)

Egypt, slavery and sanctuary (2)

55   EGYPT, LAND OF CRAFT AND CULTURE

1   Egypt, land of craft and culture,
　　skill and science, script and art;
　　wealth and beauty by the river,
　　life-sustaining through its heart.

2   Egypt, land of need and crisis,
　　famine blighting ancient years;
　　God has sent his servant Joseph,
　　sharing food and calming fears.

3   Egypt, land of death and terror,
　　bitter toil and slavery;
　　Moses, one unlikely saviour,
　　leads to freedom through the sea.

4   Egypt, land of war and struggle,
　　doubtful ally, fickle friend;
　　neighbours come to fear her folly,
　　prophets see her triumphs end.

5   Egypt, land of hope and refuge
　　in the days of Herod's power,
　　gives to Christ a vital welcome,
　　safety at the crucial hour.

6   Culture, crisis, terror, struggle,
　　hope for travellers, help at home:
　　where the word of God is planted,
　　Egypt sees his kingdom come.

7   Shining Sun and living Water,
　　Jesus, King at God's right hand,
　　let the glory of your gospel
　　bless this people, save this land!

8787   Tune: STUTTGART

Scriptures: Gen 12:10–20; 41, 45, 47　　Exod 1–2, 14–15　　Deut 23:7　　2 Kgs 18:21　　Isa 31:1–3
Jer 42:13–22　　Hos 11　　Mal 4:2　　John 4:1–14　　Matt 2:13–23

Written: Herne Hill, SE London, 8 November 2015

This hymn grew out of, and on the day after, No.54, 'The land of pyramids and palms' (q.v.), and a sense that that was on the long side. Written mainly in the early hours of Sunday Nov 8th, with Egypt much in the weekend's news, it consisted originally of three stanzas (the eventual 2, 3 and 5, all much-revised). But these seemed woefully incomplete, particularly at both ends; as so often, then, the text grew well beyond my first intentions. With stanza 4 added to reflect the prophets' warnings about Egypt as a dangerous world power and unreliable neighbour (Isaiah 31, Hosea 11), it ended with 152 words; a slight improvement on the 164 of its 'parent' hymn! (For comparison, 'The Lord's my shepherd' has 114, 'Our God our help in ages past', usual version, 135.)

A fair question: When might this be sung? **Answer:** Whenever special prayer is made for Egypt, where sun and water have historically been deified (see verse 7).

Matthew 7:24–29
Hearing and obeying

56 THE WISE MAN BUILT… WHEN JESUS FINISHED ALL HE HAD TO SAY

1 The wise man built his house upon the rock…

2 The foolish man built his house upon the sand…

3 When Jesus finished all he had to say,
the crowds were filled with wonder on the day;
he calls on everybody to obey—
there's no-one else like him!
So when he speaks and you can hear, hear, hear,
then don't be foolish when it's clear, clear, clear;
be wise enough to use your ear, ear, ear,
then do just what he says!

Tune, and text of verses 1-2, traditional

Scriptures: Matt 7:24–29 Jas 1:22
Written (final version): Bromley, Kent, 2009
How dare we tamper with, or in this case add to, the classic and well-loved texts of past generations? In this case, 'only' a favourite (and 20th century) children's song, but one which, while based firmly on the words of Jesus which bring the Sermon on the Mount to its challenging close, does not go so far as saying what our Lord is actually talking about! For some years this bothered me; when using it with children and enjoying the fun element, I always tried to explain what it was all about—that is, not just about house-building. So my additional and third stanza, remaining in draft form for some time, finally took this shape, not without advice from friends, towards the end of 2009. It made its debut at Hayes Lane Baptist Church (Family Service) in Feb 2011.

Mark's Gospel
The urgent evangelist

57   JOHN MARK WHO PENNED HIS MASTER'S LIFE

1 John Mark who penned his Master's life,
   his mighty works and urgent words:
   a gospel man from first to last,
   he showed the glory is the Lord's.

2 His one false step we clearly know,
   for he was frail, as we have been;
   but then by grace regained the path
   to join in travels unforeseen.

3 His pages bring us face to face
   with One who serves, and pays the price;
   the Son of Man, the Son of God,
   a pattern and a sacrifice:

4. Our teaching, healing, saving Christ,
   betrayed, condemned and lifted up,
   at last forsaken, and for us
   he cried aloud, and drank the cup.

5 With Peter, Barnabas and Paul,
   let Mark still play his vital part
   in preaching him who died, but lives,
   and speaks to every human heart.

6. God grant us, as we read his book,
   the opened eye, the listening ear;
   till sun grows dark and stars shall fall,
   and worlds shall see the Lord appear.

LM   Tune: GONFALON ROYAL

Scriptures: Mark's Gospel passim: Acts 12:12; 13:5,13; 15:36–39   2 Tim 4:11   1 Pet 5:13
Written: Herne Hill, SE London, Feb-Dec 2017.
At different levels I have been enriched by three varied churches dedicated to Mark the evangelist; at Bromley as a boy, Biggin Hill as a teenager, Barrow-in-Furness as a curate. London connections have included those at Old Ford (E9) and Kennington (SE11). So maybe it is time (I thought) for a hymn reflecting the special role of this disciple in the New Testament. This text took me most of the year to complete.

Mark 1:14–20 (one)
Repenting, believing, obeying (1)

58 REPENT! THIS IS THE GOSPEL CALL

1 Repent! This is the gospel call;
  to stop, to think, to change:
  no hope we had, no life at all,
  and God to us was strange.

2 How could we change without God's grace,
  to take our minds in hand?
  He knew our need, he met our case
  and gave us faith to stand.

3 In us there was no good, until
  in love for us he came;
  we said, 'I can, I shall, I will!'
  and called upon his name.

4 That name which echoes down the years
  is Jesus Christ, the Lord:
  the King who takes our sins and fears,
  believed, obeyed, adored.

CM   Tune: IRISH

Scriptures: Ps 34:4–6   Mark 1:14–15   Acts 2:21,38; 4:12; 5:31; 11:18; 20:21   Rom 2:4   2 Tim 2:25
Written: Herne Hill, SE London, 13–17 Feb 2016
From time to time someone claims that the call to repent is a missing theme from our presentation of the Christian gospel; they are often right. It is also right to remind ourselves first, that repentance is essential and second, that it is the gift of God. No particular event prompted me to express this in verse; but I continue to be conscious that many expressions of the faith, spoken or sung, tend to marginalise or omit this painful but vital demand. Its theme was the opening salvo of the Reformation, no.1 of Martin Luther's '95 Theses' of which the 500th anniversary was celebrated in 2017.

Mark 1:14–20 (two)

Repenting, believing, obeying—(2) (Lakeside then and now)

59 THE STORY'S NEVER QUITE COMPLETE

1 The story's never quite complete
　　without the blue lakeside:
　the Psalms give us a preview;
　　the Good Shepherd is our guide.
　He leads me by still waters
　　and green pastures where I feed;
　how therefore can I lack one thing
　　of what I truly need?

2 And when the Son of God appears
　　to call the fishermen
　we trace his feet through Palestine
　　beside the lake again.
　He calls those first disciples
　　and his word is 'Follow me',
　and listen! He still summons us
　　from that fair Galilee.

3 For three years he is teaching,
　　warning what is bound to come;
　he loves this earth and people,
　　but this world is not his home.
　They seized and stripped and tortured
　　him, did to him all they could,
　and at the end they nailed him high
　　upon a cross of wood.

4 But that is not the final scene,
　　as he himself has said;
　how slow we are grasp it—
　　he is risen from the dead!
　He finds them in the garden,
　　or he joins them in the lane;
　he eats with them at table,
　　and what joy is theirs again!

5 So we today can meet him still,
　　in street or close or drive,
　at supper, lunch or breakfast-time:
　　this Jesus is alive!
　In some surprising places comes
　　this Friend who once has died,
　in garden, hillside, city, town,
　　or by our own lakeside.

14 14 14 14　　Tune: LAKESIDE by William Hallworth (2007)

Scriptures: Ps 23:1–3; 34:9–10　　Mark 1:14–18; 8:31; and 15　　Luke 24:1–35　　　　John 13:34; 16:28; 19:41–20:17; 21:1–14　　1 Cor 15:20

Written: Bromley, Kent, 2007

Not originally written as a hymn, but one of a short series 'Know Your Parish' written for the church magazine of Holy Trinity Bromley Common, based on road-names in the neighbourhood (Narrow Way, Cross Road, Trinity Close etc). This was the 'Lakeside Drive' item, and is included here because my accordion-playing neighbour William Hallworth (of nearby Gravel Road) was moved to compose a tune for it.

Mark 4:1–2

He taught them many things

60 OUR TEACHER AND MASTER, REDEEMER AND LORD

1 Our Teacher and Master, Redeemer
     and Lord,
   still teach us today by your Spirit and
     word;
   forgive us our slowness to learn and
     obey,
   and open our hearts to receive what
     you say.

2 You taught on the hillside, you taught
     by the sea,
   you spoke to five thousand, to twelve
     or to three;
   in temple and synagogue, village and
     town,
   at sunrise and noon, and at sun's going
     down.

3 You taught us of judgement, of heaven
     and hell,
   of what it will cost if we choose to
     rebel:
   you brought the good news, and the
     call to repent;
   you showed us the Father, by whom
     you were sent.

4 You taught us forgiveness, and trust for
     our food;
   to love those who hate us, to pray for
     their good:
   the danger of riches, of violence and
     greed;
   the blessing of sharing with neigh-
     bours in need.

5 You taught by your life and you taught
     by your death;
   you spoke from the cross as you spent
     your last breath:
   at lakeside and pathway and breaking
     of bread
   you taught from the Scriptures, alive
     from the dead.

6 Our Teacher and Master, Redeemer
     and Lord,
   still teach us, we pray, by your Spirit
     and word,
   to learn of your wisdom and grow in
     your grace,
   till darkness is gone, and we see face
     to face.

Praise Trust   11 11 11 11   Tune: ST DENIO

Scriptures: A great many, in all four Gospels

Written: Herne Hill, SE London, August 2015

Prompted by what seemed an overloading of Sunday morning with modern songs about the cross; very necessary, but virtually none of them recognised the three years of teaching ministry which led up to it, and indeed followed! See also nos.50 and 51; this text is the result of severely pruning a first version of 40 lines.

Mark 4:35–41

We are witnesses of all that he did

61 THE LORD WHO CALMED THE WAVES

1 The Lord who calmed the waves
    by his compelling word
can master us, and saves;
    let his command be heard!
As Galilee once knew his voice,
so in his peace let us rejoice.
    Yes, Lord, you calm the waves;
    today you calm the waves.

2 The Lord who healed the lame,
    and set them on their feet,
still speaks to us by name,
    to make our faith complete.
The ills of body, mind and soul
he knows, and loves to make us whole.
    Yes, Lord, you heal the lame;
    today you heal the lame.

3 The Lord who freed the slaves
    of money, power and pride,
what fame or folly craves
    he dealt with and defied;
and all the world's imagined wealth
could never lead to life and health.
    Yes, Lord, you free the slaves;
    today you free the slaves.

4 The Lord who raised the dead
    can breathe new life today;
himself our living Head
    to follow and obey.
When we were helpless, loveless, lost,
he brought us hope and bore the cost.
    Yes, Lord, you raise the dead;
    today you raise the dead.

5 The Lord who suffered pain
    in agony alone,
is risen now to reign
    and make his kingdom known.
Christ Jesus, you make all things new,
so let us die and rise with you.
    Yes, Lord, we live in you;
    Amen! We live in you.

6666 8866 Tune: DIVINE MYSTERIES

Scriptures: Mt 9:9–13 Mk 2:1–12;4:35–41 Lk 7:11–17;19:1–10; 24:45–48 Jn 8:31–36
Written: Herne Hill, SE London, March–April 2017. To adopt a tune with other associations for a further celebration of the Lord's ministry, then and now; see notes to nos.50, 51, 59 and 60.

Luke 1:26–38

Christmas with the Holy Trinity

62 FATHER GOD, ON THIS DARK NIGHT

1 Father God, on this dark night shine
    your light,
melt our hearts, restore our sight!
    You have sent, beyond our dreaming,
    your dear Son for our redeeming;
for this Gift of gifts we praise
God who made this day of days.

2 Holy Spirit, you have come, finding room,
to a favoured virgin's womb,
    Mary listened, truth believing,
    Christ the Holy One conceiving;
so today from Scripture's word
your life-giving voice is heard.

3 Jesus Christ the tiny one, firstborn
    Son,
what a work must now be done!
    What a doubtful welcome waiting,
    what a stir you are creating –
manger bed and thorny crown
turning this world upside down!

4 Sovereign, Holy Trinity, glory be
to the eternal One-in-Three!
    Praise for love that found and saved us
    from the sins that long enslaved us;
thanks for this, one Christmas more,
space to meet, respond, adore.

737 8877   Tune: ROCKING

Scriptures: Matt 1: 20–21   Luke 1:26–38 and 2   1 Tim 1:5
Written: Bromley, Kent, 17–21 November 2008
A Trinitarian hymn written for my parish church of Holy Trinity Bromley Common, for the carol service in 2008, at the invitation of the vicar Roger Bristow. Here, I felt, was a still-familiar tune usually wedded to unusable words.

Luke 2:1–7 (one)

Christmas light

63   ILLUMINATIONS ON

1   Illuminations on!
Festivities, begin!
    When tower bells sound
    their timely round
we can't help joining in!

2   Imprinted on our hearts,
this news that seemed so strange:
    a tiny head,
    a manger bed,
a world which Christ will change!

3   Immanuel his name:
God walks with us on earth;
    today our theme
    is Bethlehem,
and one momentous birth.

4   Immortal love has come
before our mortal sight;
    the promised King
    who comes to bring
both danger and delight.

5   Incarnate God, you give
salvation from our sin;
    and as your call
    extends to all,
we can't help joining in!

66446 (SM) Tunes: KEMSING, by Brian Raynor (2009);
ILLUMINATIONS, by Jonathan Gooch (2011)

Scriptures: Matt 1:23; 2:1–6   Luke 2:1–7, 34   John 1:14   Acts 17:6
Written: Bromley, Kent, September 2009
The words were written at the first composer's request to his existing tune, for the Kemsing Singers' annual Carol Concert in December 2009. Another requirement was to start with the letter 'I' to fit into an alphabetical sequence spelling out the word 'Christmas'. To be extra sure I made every verse begin in that way, resisting the first-person-singular pronoun!

Heavy snow and treacherous ice (so nice on the cards and calendars) severely reduced the numbers of both audience and choir; the ailing Brian Raynor was unable to attend, and only the first two stanzas were sung, with a sense of unpreparedness and anti-climax. So on their debut, neither the music nor the message (let alone the final stanza) made much of an impact. Sadly, Brian died in May 2011. Jonathan Gooch composed a new tune for inclusion as a solo in the Christmas concert at Horsham (see no.53) in December that year.

Luke 2:1–7 (two)

Seasonal questions and answers

64 CAN THIS BE THE TOWN

1 Can this be the town
of all the special places
located on the map,
where God has made his home?
    Yes, Lord! We are here
    to welcome your arrival.

2 Can this be the date
of all the many highlights
included on the plan,
when God has come to birth?
    Yes, Lord! We have come
    to find your free forgiveness.

3 Can this be the hour
of all the vital moments
recorded on the clock,
when God is seen on earth?
    Yes, Lord! We can trust
    your grace which is for ever.

4 Can this be the One
of all the chosen prophets
declared to be the Son,
the Saviour of the world?
    Jesus! We shall run
    to witness to your glory.

576657 Tune by Elspeth Thompson

Scriptures: Luke 2:1–7 John 1:14; 4:42 Gal 4:4–5
Written: Bromley, Kent, 29 Dec 2008, revised 8 April 2009.
Another Christmas text written with the Kemsing Singers in mind (see no.63) but which did not prove suitable. 'Too many questions?' wondered another musical friend; but not if they help to highlight the answers!

Luke 2:1–20 (one)
Surprises

65 IF CHRISTMAS TAKES US ALL BY SURPRISE

1 If Christmas takes us all by surprise
when every year gives time to prepare,
those shepherds might have something
    to say
and wise men, too, recalling the day
of opened treasures, opened eyes,
when they became more truly wise.

2 If Christmas costs far more than we
    planned,
in time and lights and travel and gifts,
let Joseph, Mary, offer a word,
the price they paid, the promise they
    heard,
and we might start to understand
our wealth from God's most lavish
    hand.

3 If Christmas leaves us worse than be-
    fore,
to whom God speaks and works for our
    good,
in anxious mind or troublesome days,
reluctant moments spared for his praise:
where Scripture points, let us explore;
where angels sing, let us adore.

4 Let God surprise with joy that he gives;
be Spirit-filled and eager to grow,
and gladly meet the end of the year
with news to share with everyone here:
that Christ was born, has died, but lives;
each one who comes, the Christ re-
    ceives.

9999 88   new tune needed

Scriptures: Matthew 2   Luke 2
Written: Portsmouth–Bromley train, 5–6 Nov 2011, small revisions 20 Nov.
For the background, see the notes to no.53; on my way back from two days with my son Jonathan and family on the Isle of Wight, this was another attempt to meet the needs of the Horsham event. Ironically in view of stanza 1, an email from Steve Piggott was waiting for me at home, beginning, 'Christmas is rushing up on us…'! (Is it really?)

Luke 2:1–20 (two)

The news gets around

66   FOR COUNTLESS MILLIONS YET TO HEAR

1   For countless millions yet to hear
of manger bed or midnight clear,
of herald angels, David's town:
Lord, help us show how Love came down.

2   For any weary of the song
of future peace or present wrong,
renew their wonder at this Child,
in God and sinners reconciled.

3   For all forbidden now to sing
the praise of Christ, the new-born King,
the infant holy, sinless boy:
give them fresh hope and Christmas joy.

4   For youngest ones who sing this day
their first Nowells, that bed of hay,
now may they love what then you gave:
the Prince of glory, born to save.

5   For some who can no longer cope
with ancient scroll or promised hope,
or frankincense and myrrh and gold:
grant them new treasures from the old.

6   For friends who soon will sing no more
on earth, their 'Come, let us adore',
draw near, as they approach the throng,
the 'Gloria' of heaven's song.

7   Until that Day, we join to bless
his name, the Sun of righteousness,
and find in him this day, this night,
the God from God, the Light from Light.

LM   Tune: SOLOTHURN

Scriptures: Mal 4:2   Matt 1:18–25; 2:1–12   Luke 1:26–38; 2:1–20   Rom 5:8–11   1 John 3:5
Rev 5:13
Written: Bromley, Kent, 18–26 November 2008
A rather specialist text? Woven into my stanzas are phrases from some nine traditional carols and two contemporary ones (a good exercise: try spotting them!). The singers don't need to know that, as I hope the text still makes sense in itself.

Luke 2:29

Departing in peace

67   LORD, IN YOUR HAND IS EVERY LIFE

1   Lord, in your hand is every life,
    our heartbeat, senses, blood and breath;
    our bodies and our minds you know,
    our day of birth, our day of death.

2   For all who near the end of life
    and those who serve and care for them,
    to you we pray, in love draw near,
    as once you neared Jerusalem.

3   For all who dread the end of life,
    your word is 'Do not be afraid';
    we pray that they may turn and trust,
    have sins forgiven, fears allayed.

4   For all who crave the end of life,
    when pain or grief are all they find,
    we pray for them the gift of hope,
    release in calm and peace of mind.

5   For all who face the end of life
    with steadfast confidence in you,
    we give you thanks, our risen Lord;
    grant us such faith and comfort too.

Praise Trust LM   Tune: BRESLAU

Scriptures: Gen 49:29–33; 50:24–26   Deut 34:1–8   Luke 2:29   John 11:25–26   Acts 7:54–60
1 Cor 15:50–58   Phil 1:21   2 Tim 4:6–8
Written: Sydenham and Herne Hill, SE London, Feb and Sept 2016, Jan 2017
Thirteen years after my dear Marjorie died, I visited St Christopher's Hospice in Sydenham where her earthly days ended in 2003, as I sometimes did on this anniversary. Thinking of those in that place of skilful, loving care who would soon be facing their Maker, as well as friends who had recently died, their families and carers, I put some thoughts and prayers into these verses for possible use as a hymn. It would probably be sung, if at all, by the healthy rather than the dying. In response to friendly comments a new first stanza was added, another replaced, and the original last one dropped.

Luke 2:41–50

Asking questions

68 SOME CAME TO CHRIST LONGING FOR BLESSING

1 Some came to Christ longing for blessing:
'Hear us and help us'; 'Please come to heal'.
None was rejected, none was passed over;
all the five thousand shared in his meal.

2 Some came to Christ bursting with questions:
'Why do we suffer?' 'When will this be?'
'Where do you come from?' 'How can you
      prove it?'
'What about Moses?' 'What about me?'

3 Dear listening Lord, you too have questions:
'Why are you anxious?' 'Have you not read?'
'Who was the neighbour?' 'Who are my
      brothers?'
'Why don't you think God raises the dead?'

4 'Where is your faith? Why are you fearful?'
'Do you believe I can make you whole?'
'What is the good in gaining the whole world,
then lose your true life, forfeit your soul?'

5 Every new day brought near that evening
when evil powers closed in for the kill.
Seized and betrayed, then beaten and
      blood-stained
still he faced questions, asking them still.

6 'Are you a king? Can you not hear us?
Have you no answer—not even one?'
'Why come with weapons? Who can
      accuse me?
Why do you beat me? What have I done?'

7 Lord Jesus Christ, risen and reigning,
question us, change us, search through and through.
Teach us to ask how best we can serve you,
making disciples, faithful to you.

9 9 10 9 (distinctive)   new tune needed

Scriptures: A good exercise to supply them, from all four Gospels!
Questions to Jesus, e.g. Matt 16:1   Mark 11:28   Luke 18:28   John 2:18   etc
Questions from Jesus, e.g. Matt 6:27–28   Mark 3:33   Luke 8:25   John 5:6   etc
Both: Luke 2:41–50
Written: Herne Hill, SE London, Aug 2013 and July 2015
Much is written and preached about the commands and promises of Scripture; much less it seems about its questions, notably in the Gospels. We could add many from the book of Job or the Psalms, but there must be a limit somewhere. In 2013 I had made some notes for a hymn-text on this theme, and nearly two years later worked them into this version.

Trees along the River

Luke 7:31–36
You can't please everyone

69   WE PLAYED THE FLUTE, THEY DID NOT DANCE

1 We played the flute, they did not dance;
we cried, they did not grieve;
whatever reasons we advance
this world will not believe.

2 For John was known to fast and pray
and trod his path alone,
while Jesus ate and drank each day
with people of the town.

3 Only God's Spirit can convince
the human heart and mind
which still bear God's true fingerprints,
that all who seek may find.

4 While those in chains of unbelief
will never lack excuse,
but cannot see their coming grief
because of how they choose.

5 Yet, Lord, your warnings still ring true
for love of those who hear;
so help us live and speak for you
always and everywhere.

6 Forgive us when the fault is ours,
things poorly done or said;
break through in grace and sovereign
power,
and come to wake the dead.

CM   Tune: LONDON NEW

Scriptures: Matt 11:16–19   Luke 7:31–36   John 16:7–11   Eph 2:4–5
Written: at or around Bromley, Kent; March 2010 and July–Sept 2012
A better title could be 'Resistance to the Gospel'. Among several texts which I had in embryonic or draft form from Spring 2010, and set about finalising more than two years later, this proved the most difficult (and therefore the last) to get right or trim into shape. Some of the earlier ideas and lines were worked out on various local train and bus journeys.

Luke 9: 57–62

Son of Man; his own favourite title

70   JESUS, SON OF MAN, TRAVELLING THIS EARTH

1   Jesus, Son of Man,
    travelling this earth,
pathways with nowhere to lay your head:
teach us to walk closely with you,
following the kingdom's call.

2   Prophet, Son of Man,
    speaking what is right,
never may we be ashamed of you:
nor of your name, nor of your words,
through our fleeting mortal days.

3   Priest and Son of Man,
    lifted from the earth,
high on the terrible cross of wood:
by your great love, by your life-blood,
drawing nations to yourself.

4   King and Son of Man,
    coming on the clouds,
every sure promise fulfilled in you:
may we endure, let us not fail,
when you look for faith on earth.

5   Christ and Son of Man,
    Rescuer and Judge,
for all your works and for all your words,
all that you are: Hallelujah,
glory be to God: Amen!

Tune: WE SHALL OVERCOME

Scriptures by stanza: (1) Luke 9:57-62   Mark 8:34-38   (2) Mark 8:31; 18:8   (3) John 3:14–16; 12:32-34   (4) Mark 13:26-27   Luke 18:8   (5) Matt 25:31-33
Written: Herne Hill, SE London; Kendal, Cumbria; and train between, June 2015.
Preparing a sermon on 'The Son of Man', Brian Edwards asked me about hymns on the subject. Although this is the most frequently-used title of Jesus in the four Gospels, almost always on his own lips, very few hymns explore it in detail. Brian sent a copy of his sermon, hinting at a job for me; the resulting text was drafted mainly on the train, and later reduced from ten stanzas to five.

Luke 24:1

The new beginning

71 VERY EARLY, SUNDAY MORNING

[Chorus:]
Sing glory glory, Hallelujah!
Hallelujah to the King!
Sing glory glory, Hallelujah!
Christ is risen, so let us sing:

1 Very early, Sunday morning
   Jesus rose up from his grave;
   every Sunday we remember,
   we're the ones he came to save.

[Chorus]

2 Thank you, Jesus, Lord and Saviour,
   that you gave your life for me;
   once you died but now you're living
   by your Easter victory.

[Chorus]

Tune: SING GLORY, GLORY (traditional)

Scriptures: Matt 28:1–7   Mark 16:1–7   Luke 24:1–7   John 20:1   Gal 2:20   1 Tim 1:15
Rev 1:18
Written: Bromley, Kent, April 2012
The chorus is anonymous, and appears in *Church Family Worship* (1986). The verses were added for the
'Messy Church' Easter celebration at Holy Trinity Church, Bromley Common, accompanied by George
Collett on guitar and some enthusiastic younger children with the shakers they had made that afternoon.

John 1:1–14

The eternal Word

72 CHRIST THE WORD, ETERNAL ONE

1 Christ the Word, eternal One,
speech before all words began,
everlasting royal Son,
God of God, becoming Man:
  Christ, in you all things were made,
  pure in majesty arrayed.

2 Christ our Joy, revealing One,
giving life, creating light,
shining like the morning sun
overcoming deepest night:
  grant us in your sovereignty
  ears to hear and eyes to see.

3 Christ our Hope, the promised One,
prophets saw your coming reign:
what was written, you have done;
what was spoken shall remain.
  Theirs the witness we receive,
  yours the gospel we believe.

4 Christ the King, rejected One,
humble, coming to your own,
seeking all, refusing none,
yet unwelcome and unknown:
  judged, and lifted up to die,
  buried, you are raised on high.

5 Christ the Life, the saving One,
calling while it is today,
shown as God's beloved Son,
Lamb who takes our sin away:
  all whose trust is in your name
  never shall be put to shame.

6 Christ the Lord, all-glorious One,
pitched your tent upon this earth;
here was life for us begun,
gift of God by second birth:
  now you reign in highest place,
  Saviour, full of truth and grace.

77 77 77   Tune: RATISBON

Scriptures: Matt 3:17; 17:5; 24:35   Luke 24:45   John 1:29; 3:3-15; 6:37; 8:28; 12:32-33
1 Cor 15:3-4   Phil 2:5-11   Col 1:16-17   Heb 3:13   1 Pet 1:23; 2:6   Rev 1:16
Written: Herne Hill, SE London, 3–4 Jan 2016. One Sunday evening in January 2016, on a visit to All
Souls' Church, Langham Place, I was moved by David Turner's sermon on John 1:1–14, with six headings,
each one a title for our Lord based on these verses. This hymn keeps the same structure and much of the
same wording. The suggested tune may help my text from its association with Charles Wesley's 'Christ
whose glory fills the skies'; but I am open to other suggestions (old or new), if they are brisk and positive.

John 16:12–15
The chief work of the Holy Spirit

73   HOLY SPIRIT, SHOW US JESUS

1   Holy Spirit, show us Jesus
through the Scriptures we can know;
yours the light which brings true
wisdom,
yours the seed from which we grow.

2   Holy Spirit, make Christ Jesus
centre of our heart and mind;
word of truth and life of beauty,
prize that all who seek shall find.

3   Holy Spirit, let King Jesus
speak as once before he spoke;
when the deaf and blind responded,
lost were found and dead awoke.

4   Holy Spirit, keep this Jesus
loved as Saviour, served as Lord;
granting gifts within one body,
ruling lives he has restored.

5   Holy Spirit, may our Jesus
probe into our inmost need;
judging wrong, exalting goodness,
guiding all whom grace has freed.

6   Holy Spirit, breath of Jesus,
living water, flowing stream,
his the everlasting honour,
highest glory, praise supreme.

7   Holy Spirit, fire of Jesus,
may we catch the sacred flame;
shining, burning, ever-growing,
so the world can hear his name.

8787   Tune: CROSS OF JESUS

Scriptures: John 14:26; 15:26; 16:14 and the four Gospels, passim

Written: Herne Hill, SE London, May 2016

On the evening of Whitsunday (Pentecost) 2016, I attended a London church where the theme of the service was 'the Spirit of Truth'. His main work, said the preacher, drawing on John chs.14–16, was and is to reveal to us the Lord Jesus Christ. Fine! So it seemed strange that while the first of five hymns and songs included the word 'Christ', none mentioned Jesus by name. When I commented on this afterwards, the Minister suggested that I should write a hymn to make up for it. Whether he was serious or not (for such half-teasing invitations often come my way), this is what I tried to do over the next ten days.

John 19:14

Here is your king!

74 LET US FIRST SING OF BETHLEHEM'S BABY

1 Let us first sing of Bethlehem's baby,
unnoticed, dependent and small:
our God is revealed in a manger;
and Glory is born for us all.
　　For all this and more, let us sing;
　　but most, of how Christ is the King.

2 Let us sing of hard Nazareth's Teacher,
whose words will take root in the mind;
the stories that end with a question,
the challenge to seek and to find.
　　For all this and more…

3 Let us sing of far Galilee's Healer,
whose love will turn no-one away;
for those on the edge or the outside
are welcome to enter and stay.
　　For all this and more…

4 Let us sing of good Bethany's Giver,
the true way of living made plain;
the path and the pattern to follow,
for walking in peace or in pain.
　　For all this and more…

5 Let us sing of Gethsemane's Master,
the garden of learning and loss;
where praying leads on to betrayal,
as Jesus moves nearer the cross.
　　For all this and more…

6 Let us sing of that death in the darkness,
when truth is nailed up on a tree;
Jerusalem comes to its judgement,
but we are forgiven and free.
　　For all this and more…

7 Let us sing of the morning of triumph,
the life-giving power of the Name;
from heaven the Kingdom is coming
and earth is no longer the same.
　　For all this and more…

10 8 9 8 8 8　　new tune needed

Scripture chapters: Mark 3, 14 and 15　　Luke 2, 4 and 13　　John 20 and 21.
Written: Herne Hill, SE London, Sept 2015–April 2016
Influenced partly by the writings of Bishop Tom Wright, I began on a text celebrating how 'God became king'. But then, God is, always was and will be the King; so, '…how God is the King'? But the overwhelming New Testament emphasis is that Christ is the King, including his own claims (e.g. John 18:37)! So the re-frain took its present shape, after I had gradually built up the stanzas to include both the traditional themes and some of those often sidelined.

John 19:38-42

God is not absent

75   CAN GOD BE WITH THE BROTHERS

1   Can God be with the brothers
who take Christ's body down,
and step into the limelight
as darkness grips the town?
>   Yes, God is with his people
>   who dare do something new,
>   with courage to accomplish
>   what no-one else can do.

2   Can God be with the sisters
preparing costly spice,
to sweeten bitter moments
of loss and sacrifice?
>   Yes, God is with his people
>   who lovingly press on
>   with gifts of special fragrance,
>   when hope has nearly gone.

3   Can God be with disciples
who take the time to rest,
who learn to wait in patience
when quietness is best?
>   Yes, God is with his people
>   who make his word their choice,
>   and in the Sabbath stillness
>   are open to his voice.

4   Can God be with the doubters
who run to check the grave,
whose minds are full of questions
before an empty cave?
>   Yes, God is with his people,
>   and will not turn away
>   the ones who greet the morning
>   of resurrection-day.

Praise Trust   7676D   Tune: PASSION CHORALE

Scriptures: John 19:38-42; 20:1-18   Luke 23:55-56
Written: Herne Hill, SE London, March and July 2015
A reaction against a hymn saying that at the cross 'now God departs'. We must give the cry of dereliction its full weight, but he is still there at Luke 23:46.

John 19:38–20:18

Buried and raised

76   THE REALM OF OUR MUCH-TRAVELLED LORD

1   The realm of our much-travelled Lord
surrounds us here, below, above;
to him no land is unexplored,
no strange domain beyond his love.

2   For he has gone where none before
has reached, where paths are his alone;
no arms have felt the weight he bore,
no feet have deeper chasms known.

3   Dear silent Lord, in one far grave
once you were lying, still and cold,
when followers fled and foes grew brave,
and one false heart the truth had sold.

4   But here and there, half out of sight,
two men, three women, neighbour, friend,
did what they could before the night,
before the day, before the end.

5   Let us, like them, come, face this death
to find where new beginnings lie
for where was once no life, no breath,
one grave lies open to the sky.

6   And two or three, eleven, a score,
hundreds and thousands soon shall come,
together singing evermore
the risen Christ, the conquered tomb.

LM   Tune: CHURCH TRIUMPHANT

Scriptures: Matt 27:57–28:19   Mark 15:42–16:8   Luke 23:50–24:12   John 19:38–20:18
1 Cor 15:1–8

Written: Oakley, Suffolk, spring/summer 1995.

In November 2009 I unearthed this item which I had regarded as a poem (or at least verses) when I wrote it during our last summer in rural Oakley, not long before we moved back to inner-London. So it was not included in either *Light upon the River* (1998) or *Walking by the River* (2008). Since then, however, it has seemed to me that many such verses gain publication and recognition also as congregational hymns. So at that point this one was transferred from my file of verses to the collection of hymns.

John 20:19-21

Peace: the gift and the Giver

77   PEACE BE WITH YOU, JESUS SAID

1   Peace be with you, Jesus said;
   now he lives, who once was dead:
   giving peace to all his friends,
   peace that lasts and never ends.

2   Jesus calls to me and you,
   share his peace with others too;
   making peace instead of war,
   that is what we're praying for.

3   Those who make this peace somehow,
   they are called God's children now:
   Jesus knew it long before –
   one day wars will be no more.

7777   Tune: ROCKBEARE by Sue Gilmurray (2016)

Scriptures: Isa 2:4   Mic 4:3   Matt 5:9   John 14:27; 16:33; 20:19–21   Acts 10:36   Rom 5:1
Written: Herne Hill, SE London, 28 Oct 2016
What began as a children's song is probably more use as an adult hymn; it is not so simple as it may seem.
It was replaced for primary school assembly (17 November) with 'Peace with you... Jesus said... Happy
are the people... who make peace'—to FRÈRE JACQUES.

Acts 2:1–4

Pentecost song

78   HOLY SPIRIT, LIKE THE WIND

1   Holy Spirit, like the wind,
Holy Spirit, like the wind,
Holy Spirit, like the wind,
Come and breathe on me.

2   Holy Spirit, like the fire… (x3),
Come and burn for me.

3   Holy Spirit, like the stream… (x3),
Come and flow for me.

4   Holy Spirit, speak to me… (x3).
Show us more of Jesus.

7775 [6]: SKIP TO MY LOU (adapted); or new tune needed

Scriptures: John 3:8; 7:38–39; 14:26; 15:26; 16:13–14; Acts 2:1–4
Written: Bromley, Kent, 9 May 2011
This was another contribution to 'Messy Church' (see nos.1 and 2) when our theme was the Holy Spirit, or Pentecost. Short and simple but I hope scriptural, as it needed to be. Basic visual aids can help; I used some which I had first prepared for Poplar in the early 1970s.

Acts 2:41–42

'Baptized, and… the breaking of bread'.

79   THE SACRAMENTS JESUS HAS GIVEN US TO SHARE

1 The sacraments Jesus has given us
to share
are pledges and badges for
Christians to wear;
eternity breaks into earth's time
and space
with foretastes of glory and signs
of his grace.

2 Effective to strengthen us by his
good will,
confirming the word that he lives
for us still,
invisibly working, they meet our
true need:
his baptism to cleanse us, his supper
to feed.

3 Baptized into Christ, and distinctive
in this,
as part of the church we are publicly
his;
adopted as children, forgiven our
sin,
and sealed by his Spirit, raised up to
be clean.

4 The bread and the cup which sustain
us in faith
proclaim our redemption by
Jesus's death;
we share in his body, partake of
his blood,
we love one another and draw near
to God.

5 For Jesus is risen, alive from the
dead,
salvation completed, one Lord and
one Head;
for all who find life as the fruit of
his pain,
until he returns, what sweet
blessings remain!

6 All glory to God for his gift of
new birth
with riches from heaven, to
serve him on earth;
for washing and nourishing,
water and food,
we thank him who ceaselessly works
for our good.

11 11 11 11 Tune: MONTGOMERY

Scriptures: Matt 26:26–29; 28:18–20   Acts 2:41–42   1 Cor 11:23–26; 12:13

Written: Herne Hill, SE London, Feb 2017

For the title, see Acts chapter 2; very few hymns celebrate equally both the gospel sacraments. This one, among the last to be written for the present book, draws on the language of the Thirty-Nine Articles of Religion (from the 1662 Book of Common Prayer), notably nos. 25, 27 and 28. It benefited from comments by retired bishops Timothy Dudley-Smith and Colin Buchanan, on my early draft. I was sorry to have to drop the 'not only…but rather/also' of all three Articles, for reasons of space.

Acts 7:51–60 (one)

Christmas Day and St Stephen's Day—1

80   WE CALL HIM CHRIST, THE FIRSTBORN SON

1   We call him Christ, the Firstborn Son,
and Mary's child, God's holy One;
so for the praise of him alone
    we keep the feast of Christmas.

2   The first of all the martyr-throng
was Stephen, so he joins our song;
he prayed for those who did him wrong
    and saw the Lord of heaven.

3   A birth in distant Bethlehem,
a death in dark Jerusalem;
together we remember them
    as glory comes in winter.

4   With Stephen, praise the Son of Man!
And see fulfilled the eternal plan
in which our hope of heaven began:
    a light for dim December.

5   So let us sing what God has done
by firstborn saint, in Firstborn Son;
in all the world let everyone
    sing praise to Stephen's Saviour!

8887   Tune: EWHURST

Scriptures: Luke 1:35; 2:7   Acts 3:14; 7:51–60   Col 2:15–18   Rev 1:5
Written: Bromley, Kent, July 2012.
December 26th, Boxing Day or St Stephen's Day, rarely falls on a Sunday. When it does (2010, 2021 etc), what can we sing that celebrates both that day and the day before? That was the question posed by Roger Bristow, vicar of Holy Trinity Bromley Common, around Christmas 2010; this was then my parish church, and he invited me to attempt a hymn which would fit. This proved difficult; we were too late for 2010, but in summer 2012 I unearthed some earlier scribbled ideas and produced two approaches, one for children or 'all-age' events (see no.81, 'We thank you, God, for yesterday') and this one.

Acts 7:51–60 (two)
Christmas Day and St Stephen's Day—2

81 WE THANK YOU, GOD, FOR YESTERDAY

1 We thank you, God, for yesterday,
yes, yesterday, for Christmas Day:
for gifts to share and games to play
on Christmas Day in the morning.

2 We praise you when from far and near
the signs of faith and hope appear;
the Saviour of the world is here
on Christmas Day in the morning.

3 We thank you, God, again today
on Boxing Day, St Stephen's Day;
for Stephen shows us how to pray
on Boxing Day in the morning.

4 We praise you for the loving faith
of Stephen at the point of death;
who witnessed with his dying breath
and met a glorious morning.

5 We thank you, God, for every day,
when saints are shining, come what may,
for Christ the life, the truth, the way,
for every day in the morning.

Tune: I SAW THREE SHIPS

Scriptures: Luke 2:1–20   John 4:42; 14:6   Acts 7:51–60   1 John 4:14
Written: Bromley, Kent, 2009 and 2012
A carol for children or 'all-age' events, when Boxing Day falls on a Sunday: see notes to no.80, 'We call him Christ, the Firstborn Son,'

Acts 8:26–40

Personal evangelism

82   HOLY SPIRIT, PROMPT MY HEART

1   Holy Spirit, prompt my heart
   how to serve and where to start;
   guide my footsteps where you send,
   make me listen, help, befriend,
   whether needs are great or small,
   swift and ready at your call.

2   Holy Spirit, still you speak
   to the humble and the meek;
   all the Scriptures, line by line,
   bear the stamp of truth divine:
   let your wisdom always teach
   those whose ears your words will reach.

3   Holy Spirit, you alone
   make the Saviour, Jesus, known;
   his the suffering and disgrace,
   bruised and wounded in our place;
   ours the healing of the soul,
   his the stripes that make us whole.

4   Holy Spirit once outpoured,
   you have shown us he is Lord
   by your work we trust in Christ,
   welcomed, pardoned, saved, baptized,
   loved, adopted and set free;
   but the best is yet to be.

5   Holy Spirit, you arrange
   wonders of decisive change:
   by our witness to your love,
   born of heaven from above;
   give us faith to trust, and know
   harvests from one seed can grow.

6   Holy Spirit, ever new,
   you have given us work to do;
   travel far or serve at home,
   praying, Lord, your kingdom come:
   God from all eternity,
   bring revival—start with me!

77 77 77   Tune: WELLS or DIX

Scriptures: Isa 28:10,13; 53:4–6; 66:2   Matt 6:10   Mark 4:9,20   John 3:5–8   Acts 2:33; 8:26–40
Written: Herne Hill, SE London, 5–8 June 2016
On 5th June 2016, at a Baptism and Communion service at St Mark's Church Kennington (SE London), the vicar Stephen Coulson spoke from Acts 8, taking us pointedly through the account of Philip and the Ethiopian. Picking up the themes he took, including the crucial quotations from Isaiah 53, I put these verses together in that week, hoping it was allowable to associate the 'angel' of verse 26 with 'the Spirit of the Lord' specifically mentioned in v 39.

Acts 10:33–43 (one)
The Gospel according to Peter—1

83   IN THE PRESENCE OF GOD WE ARE GATHERED TODAY

1   In the presence of God
   we are gathered today
   to attend to each word
   that the Lord has to say.

2   For our God speaks of peace
   far and near, great and small,
   by Christ Jesus his Son
   who is Lord over all.

3   When anointed with power
   he brought troubled ones rest;
   with new healing and hope
   for the sick and oppressed.

4   He was nailed to a cross
   where he carried our sin:
   but our God raised him up;
   for the grave could not win.

5   As the king of the earth
   he will come, as he said,
   as the one who will judge
   all the living and dead.

6   By his grace we are free
   to repent and believe,
   and his kingdom is here
   for us all to receive.

7   While the moment is now
   and the time is today,
   let us heed the good news,
   and be swift to obey.

6666 anapaestic   Tune by Elspeth Thompson

Scriptures: Mark 1:15   Acts 3:15; 4:10; 10:33–43; 17:31   2 Cor 6:2   Eph 2:17   1 Pet 2:24
Written: Herne Hill, SE London, 9–22 Jan 2016
The apostle Simon Peter's address, or the evangelist Luke's summary of it, at the Caesarea home of the Roman centurion Cornelius (Acts 10), is a landmark in the spread of the gospel and the growth of the early church beyond the Jewish communities. It is also a classic statement of the essentials of Christian faith; some see it also as a concise summary of the Gospel according to Mark. Perhaps surprisingly, it does not seem to have been put into verse by hymnwriters, so here is my first attempt (see also no.84) to make it singable as well as memorable.

Acts 10:33–43 (two)
The Gospel according to Peter—2

84 OUR GOD SPEAKS OF PEACE TO GREAT AS TO SMALL

1 Our God speaks of peace to great as to small
through Jesus his Son, the Lord over all:
anointed with power, he offers his rest,
his Spirit of healing for all the oppressed.

2 Once nailed to a cross, he carried our sin;
but God raised him up—the grave could not win.
His chosen apostles could see he was real,
from walking and talking to sharing a meal.

3 With oceans to cross and dangers to face,
he sent them to preach the gospel of grace;
as King of the earth he will come, as he said,
to judge all humanity, living and dead.

4 So now let us hear, repent and believe;
forgiveness is free for all to receive.
The law and the prophets prepared for this day
which Christ has fulfilled, calling us to obey.

5 All praise to our God who speaks to us still!
The Lord Jesus Christ makes known his good will:
the word and the Spirit unite all their powers;
the glory is his, and salvation is ours.

10 10 11 11   Tune: HANOVER

Scriptures: Luke 24   Acts 10:36–43   Eph 2:17   1 Pet 2:24
Written: Herne Hill, SE London, 22–24 Jan 2016
Many metrical summaries of the essential Christian gospel have been written and sung over the centuries; this is my second attempt (see no.83) structured on the apostle Peter's words at the Caesarea home of the Roman centurion Cornelius, as summarised by Luke in Acts 10. The sequel was both dramatic and far-reaching.

Acts 20:24
The gospel of the grace of God

85   THE BEAUTY AND JOY OF THE GOSPEL OF GRACE

1   The beauty and joy of the gospel of grace
    are magnets that draw us to seek the Lord's face;
    where majesty, power and justice are found,
    and love and forgiveness and mercy abound.

2   The beauty and joy of the gospel of God
    are health and refreshment, and comfort and food;
    for Jesus fulfils what the prophets foretold,
    New Testament glories surpassing the Old.

3   The beauty and joy of the gospel of Christ
    are clearly displayed in his one sacrifice;
    from shame in his dying, nailed up on a tree,
    comes hope for the world, and for captives set free.

4   The beauty and joy of the gospel of love
    are levers that make even stony hearts move,
    and melt in the fire of his burning command,
    yet rise recreated, to live and to stand.

5   The beauty and joy of the gospel of light
    bring sunrise and dawning, the ending of night,
    for he who once died is alive evermore:
    Amen! We believe you, we love and adore.

11 11 11 11   Tune: STOWEY

Scriptures: Acts 20:24   Rom 1:1,16   Eph 1:13   1 Tim 1:11
Written: Herne Hill, SE London, March 2016
The phrase 'the beauty and joy of the gospel' was used, possibly quoted from elsewhere, in a talk by Bishop Graham Kings at Trinity House, the offices of the Southwark Diocese, in March 2016. Whatever their source, I noted down these seven words and they became the starting point for this text, written at home that weekend.

Romans 8:15–23

Redeemed and adopted

86 CHOSEN FOR ADOPTION

1 Chosen for adoption
children of God's grace,
members of one family,
in each special place;
brothers now and sisters,
equal in his sight,
one in Christ together
for his praise unite.

2 All who lack assurance
his sure word can prove;
all who claim some merit
humbled by his love:
all cry 'Abba, Father',
by one Spirit sealed;
every stain is dealt with,
all the past is healed.

3 Ransomed out of darkness
at a fearful price,
rescued and made holy
by one sacrifice;
heirs of coming beauty,
through our coming King,
long for full redemption
which that day will bring.

4 Here we serve and struggle,
grow in hope and faith,
learning how to suffer
from the saints on earth.
Victory is certain,
say the saints in heaven,
all by love adopted,
all for glory given.

6565D   Tune: CUDDESDON

Scriptures: John 15:16   Rom 8:15–23   Gal 4:4–7   Eph 1:4–14
Written: Herne Hill, SE London, 9–11 August 2016
Prompted by a church study on (biblical) adoption, based on material from Wayne Grudem; like redemption this is both a past reality and a future hope. Another very rich but possibly under-used theme?

Romans 12:9–18

Helping, caring and treasuring

87   LORD, HOW WE TREASURE HELPERS AND CARERS

1   Lord, how we treasure
helpers and carers,
neighbours and workers,
answers to prayer;
sometimes in silence
sitting beside us,
bringing a blessing
just being there.

2   Proving a Godsend,
serving with gladness
those in their last years
or in their prime;
bearing the burdens,
working or waiting,
hearing our stories,
giving their time.

3   Whether by daylight
or the long night hours,
sometimes in crisis,
sometimes in calm;
blessed in their wisdom,
skilled by their training,
trusting through weakness
on your strong arm.

4   So make us helpers
formed in your image,
patient to comfort
those in our care;
weep with the mourners,
laugh with the joyful,
willing to listen,
ready to share.

5   Help of the helpers,
Carer for carers,
God never-sleeping,
Maker and Friend,
Father of Jesus,
you never fail us,
keeping each promise
through to the end.

5554D   Tune: BUNESSAN

Scriptures: Rom 12:9–16   Gal 6:2   1 Tim 5:1–16   Tit 2:1–5   1 Pet 4:8–11

Written: Herne Hill, SE London, February 2014

Having been both carer and cared for, personally and professionally, I warmed to the suggestion made in early 2014 for a hymn on these topics. This was one of several themes which writers were invited to include, by the continuing Praise! editorial group.

1 Corinthians 13

Love never fails

88   GRANT IN US, LORD, LOVE THAT LISTENS

1   Grant in us, Lord, love that listens,
keeping an attentive mind;
quiet when we need some silence,
speaking only what is kind.

2   Grant, O God, a love that hungers,
searching Scripture as your word,
fearing, thinking, trusting, doing,
where your voice is clearly heard.

3   Grant, O God, a love that pardons,
eager in forgiving sins;
reconciling warring factions,
witnessing how meekness wins.

4   Grant, O God, a love that's humble,
gracious, gentle, self-aware;
willing to receive correction,
slow to blame and quick to share.

5   Grant, O God, a love that's growing,
keen to sense unspoken needs;
never claiming all the answers,
serving well by words and deeds.

6   Grant, O God, a love that's hidden,
feeding neither pride nor praise;
known to you, unseen by others,
giving joy in Christlike ways.

7   Grant, dear God, the love of Jesus,
costly, Spirit-filled and pure;
modelled on his death and rising,
chief of all things that endure.

8787   Tune: SUSSEX

Scriptures: 1 Cor 13   Rom 12:9   1 Tim 1:5   1 Pet 4:8
Written: Herne Hill, SE London, 3–4 July 2016
Following a sermon on 1 Corinthians 13 by Simon Dowdy at Grace Church Dulwich (SE London, origi-
nally a 'plant' from St Helen's Bishopsgate), and trying to avoid (as he did) the opposite dangers of emotion
without application, and legalism with no good news.

Ephesians 2:4–7

Rich in mercy

89   TO THOSE FOR WHOM YOU LIVED AND DIED

1   To those for whom you lived and died,
    Lord, show mercy.
To those, like you, unjustly tried,
for whom you once were crucified:
    Lord, show mercy.

2   Because you warned that you must die,
    Lord, have mercy.
Because they lifted you on high
between hard earth and darkened sky:
    Lord, have mercy.

3   Because you know our inmost heart;
    Lord, show mercy.
Because you made us from the start,
your skill creating every part,
    Lord, show mercy.

4   You know our daily smiles and tears;
    Lord, have mercy.
In all our longings, all our fears,
you know the past and future years:
    Lord, have mercy.

5   To those on earth we count most dear,
    Lord, show mercy.
To small and great, and far and near,
your will be done most gladly here;
    Lord show mercy.

6   Because you never stooped to sin,
    Lord, have mercy.
Because you welcome sinners in,
and all our hopes in you begin;
    Lord, have mercy.

7   Because you met us in our need,
    rich in mercy!
As now for us you intercede,
your gift is love, and life indeed,
    glorious mercy!

84884   Tune by Elspeth Thompson

Scriptures: Ps 51:1; 139:1–6, 23   Matt 6:10   Mark 8:31   Luke 15:1–2; 18:13   John 12:32–33
Eph 2:4–7   Rom 8:34   1 Pet 2:22
Written: Herne Hill, SE London, May 2016
An anonymous printed prayer focusing on the mercy of God was the prompting for what began as a versification of its phrases, but then grew beyond its parent text.

Ephesians 2:8

By grace

90   GRACE IS THE GIFT THAT GOD ALONE

1   Grace is the gift that God alone
provides in Christ his Son;
unearned and free and undeserved
and by his suffering won.

2   Grace is the mark of all God's words,
our creed, our prayers, our songs;
we hear and speak his truth, and give
all praise where it belongs.

3   Grace is the news we have to share,
God's power for us today,
when all can hear its promises
and none is turned away.

4   Grace be with all who love our Lord
and peace within this place;
our present joy, our glorious hope,
one God of saving grace.

CM with repeats   Tune: ANTIOCH

Scriptures: Acts 15:11; 20:24   2 Cor 8:9   Eph 2:8
Written: Herne Hill, SE London, April-Dec 2015
When Grace Church Dulwich (see no.88) was ten years old in 2015, I had belonged for just over two years, since my move to Herne Hill in June 2013. I offered this hymn to mark the occasion, but it did not prove suitable.

Philippians 1:3–6

Church landmarks or anniversaries

91   FROM SMALL BEGINNINGS IN THE PAST

1 From small beginnings in the past,
for those who planned and built to last,
who followed Christ, the Way;
for those with hope who pioneered,
who kept the faith and persevered,
we praise our God today.

2 They grew by serving, being served,
in loving and in being loved,
forgiving and forgiven;
in Scripture's truth they learned and taught,
in songs of wisdom which they brought
we catch the sounds of heaven.

3 For what we now are called to face,
Lord, may we live and grow in grace,
your Spirit as our Guide;
to handle present joys and tears,
redeeming troubled weeks and years,
our Saviour at our side.

4 To learn your lifestyle, trace your hand
through paths we cannot understand,
but know your word is true;
along the road where you have gone,
in taking risks, in keeping on,
still we must follow you.

5 Whatever storms the future brings
we vow to serve the King of kings
through all that lies ahead;
a ransomed people, set apart
in soul and body, mind and heart,
for Christ our living Head.

6 And so we praise and pray and trust,
while this world's glories turn to dust,
and human strength is frail;
all hindrances we leave behind,
and every step we take, we find
your love will never fail.

886886   Tune: INNSBRUCK; or new tune needed

Scriptures: Acts 14:14   1 Cor 3:6–11   Eph 5:16   Phil 1:3–6   Col 3:12–17   2 Pet 3:18
Written: Herne Hill, SE London, 30 Sept—1 Oct 2015. For the 10th Birthday of Grace Church Dulwich (see no.90) I was asked to write a prayer for the congregation to use together. One draft included some phrases which seemed adaptable to rewriting as verse. It was not ready to be sung that year, but has been used elsewhere and remains available for any such local celebrations, focusing on a church's past, present and future.

Philippians 3:7–14

Priorities

92 OUR CHIEF INSPIRATION, OUR PRIMARY PURPOSE

1 Our chief inspiration,
    our primary purpose
  is knowing and loving you,
      God of us all:
  one Trinity merciful,
      holy, immortal:
  our joy is to hear and
      respond to your call.

2 Our mainspring of action,
    our constant endeavour,
  to trust in your promises,
      keep your commands:
  to serve and to suffer,
      to rise and to witness;
  to place every burden
      in your mighty hands.

3 Our daily delight,
    our unswerving direction,
  first hidden in secret,
      then openly shown:
  to worship with listening
      and pray with thanksgiving,
  to live in your presence
      and make your truth known.

4 Our prime motivation,
    our permanent challenge,
  the pages of Scripture,
      the Spirit within;
  when you are denied or opposed
      or avoided
  by us or our neighbours,
      our battles begin.

5 One Father of glory,
    one Jesus the Saviour,
  one Spirit of life giving birth
      from above:
  one God all-creating,
      redeeming, indwelling,
  all praise for your faithfulness,
      wisdom and love.

12 11 12 11   Tune: WAS LEBET, WAS SCHLEBET

Scriptures: Matt 6:33   John 3:3–8   2 Cor 10:3–5   Eph 6:12   Phil 3:7–14   1 Tim 6:13–16   Heb 12:1–3
1 Pet 5:7
Written: Herne Hill, SE London, May 2016
The opening line, from a report on the 'Mission-shaped church', was quoted at the start of a short sermon on Trinity Sunday (May 22) 2016, at St Paul's Herne Hill. The hymn text was the result of further pondering on this over the next few days, and some small changes suggested later by TAG.

Trees along the River

1 Timothy 2:1–3

Praying for the nation

93   LORD GOD, HOW SHALL OUR COUNTRY BE

1   Lord God, how shall our country be
not fearful, cruel or unjust;
but open, honest, fair, and free
from greed, corruption, lies and lust?

2   For you revealed your perfect will
that this and every nation knows
the prophecy which we fulfil
when justice like a river flows:

3   No widening of the deadly gap
that holds apart the rich and poor;
no vivid contrast on the map
to wreck the peace we're longing for.

4   We pray for leaders holding fast
to values which your laws uphold:
the name of Christ, as in the past,
and Scripture truths well-known of old.

5   For courts and counsellors to know
what builds a true community;
not passing fashions, outward show
or signs of newer slavery.

6   For goodness, mercy, kindness, health;
no bribes or bullying or worse;
no room for gods of chance or wealth
which well deserve your righteous curse.

7   And rescue us from love of power,
that pride which comes before a fall;
unknown to us the day, the hour
when Christ will come to judge us all.

8   Such blessings, Lord, we never earn;
so in your mercy hear our prayer,
that hearts will serve, and eyes discern
your kingdom coming, growing here.

LM   Tune needed

Scriptures: Scriptures: Deut 17:14–20   Psa 2:10–12; 85:1–4   Prov 16;18   Dan 4:37   Jer 29:7
Amos 5:24   Matt 22:15–22; 24:42–44   Rom 13:1–7   1 Tim 2:1–3   1 Pet 2:13–17
Written: Herne Hill, SE London, 15–23 Dec 2016
We have very few national hymns to rival 'Rejoice, O land, in God thy might', or 'Judge eternal, throned
in splendour'. I am aware of the risk of our aspirations being so general that they become mere platitudes,
or so specific that they sound like a party manifesto. But I thought the risk worth taking, even though it is
easier to list the dangers than the goals.

2 Timothy 1:2

An apostolic greeting; grace mercy, peace

94   GRACE FOR EVERY PROJECT

1   Grace for every project,
   Lord, we need to ask;
all our varied callings,
   every testing task.
We can ask with boldness
   once we hear your call;
grace in calm or crisis,
   grace that covers all.

2   Mercy for our failures,
   setback, shame or sin;
weakness or rebellion,
   rottenness within.
Father of all mercies,
   at the cross, forgive;
teach us true repentance,
   where to look, and live.

3   Peace for all our struggles,
   every circumstance;
prayer can face the problems,
   nothing left to chance.
Apostolic greetings
   spanning time and space,
grow the Spirit's harvest:
   mercy, peace and grace.

6565D   Tune: EVELYNS

Other Scriptures: Num 21:8–9   Isa 1:6   1 Cor 7:17–24   2 Cor 1:3   Gal 5:22   Heb 4:16   2 John 3
Written: Herne Hill, SE London, 9th November 2015
'"Grace, mercy and peace". But what depths of meaning are in the words as they stand!—"grace", for every service; "mercy", for every failure; "peace", for every circumstance'. In Nov 2015 I reached these words of Canon Guy King, then vicar of Christ Church Beckenham, Kent, in his devotional commentary on 2 Timothy, *To my Son* (1944; pp.12–13). The book was a 41st birthday gift from 14-year-old Marjorie, my future wife, to her father 'Fred', whom I never knew as he died in 1954. But we both have appreciated such words and texts as these.

2 Timothy 3:16

All Scripture

95 LORD JESUS, YOU FULFIL THE LAW

1 Lord Jesus, you fulfil the Law,
   but probe far deeper, ask much more;
   the Prophets witness to your grace
   and in the Psalms we see your face;
       your Gospel speaks of sins forgiven,
       eternal life, and opened heaven.

2 This good book shaped our nation's past
   with laws that matter, truths that last;
   in history, parable and song,
   and drama sifting right from wrong,
       authentic story, telling phrase:
       for us the blessing, yours the praise.

3 Your book confronts our world today,
   shows how to live and love and pray,
   the Scriptures we believe as true
   to guide all we can be and do:
       for future days of hope or dread
       their pages light the path ahead.

4 The Father's gift, the Spirit's breath,
   shows why you died, but conquered death;
   your church which suffers as it grows
   no king nor devil overthrows:
       such words we read, and speak, and sing,
       to praise you, Lord and Christ and King!

88 88 88   Tune: ST MATTHIAS

Scriptures: Ps 1:1–2; 19:7–11; 119:1,105   Matt 5:17–20   John 10:35   2 Tim 3:15–16   Heb 4:12–13
Written: Herne Hill, SE London, 21–25 June 2016
In a conversation at London's Barbican Centre about the planning of this, my third hymn-collection, Tim Thornborough mentioned that 2016 was the 25th birthday of the Good Book Company, founded originally as St Matthias Press in 1991. The Bible is 'The Good Book', until recently widely recognised as such, but now often considered a bad book in view of its counter-cultural teaching. Half-seriously, perhaps, the idea of a celebration hymn came up, in line with several other anniversary texts marking 50, 75, 80, 100, 150 or 200 years. So why not for 25? That same week I set to work, finding myself writing in 88 88 88 metre, which led appropriately to a match with the tune ST MATTHIAS.

Hebrews 10:24–25

Energy and edge

96 LORD CHRIST WHO BRINGS ALL LIFE TO BE

1   Lord Christ who brings all life to be,
    who grants us sight and sense and breath;
    give us, we pray, the energy,
    the cutting edge of gospel faith.

2   Not safe or soft, but challenging,
    not slick or smooth, but sharp and keen;
    to feel its probing and its sting,
    then healing where the wounds have been.

3   That every time we meet to pray,
    or join as one to start the week,
    we shall be glad this is the day
    that you have made, when you will speak.

4   To know that as we hear or read,
    we can most truly meet with you;
    to ask not only what we need,
    but what we need to be, and do.

5   And may your Spirit's ministry
    as Helper, Guide and Counsellor,
    correct and stir and set us free,
    and grow by loving, more and more.

6   So shall our praise be not in vain,
    not empty sounds nor thoughtless words;
    we and our neighbours then shall gain
    and all the glory be the Lord's.

LM   Tune: FESTUS

Scriptures: Ps 118:24   Matt 6:7   John 16:5-15   Col 1:16   Heb 1:2; 4:12-13; 10:24-25
Written: London to Glasgow train, 29 April 2016
Prompted by an expression used by Bishop Graham Kings about 'the energy and edge of the Gospel';
Graham had been a placement student at Limehouse in the 1980s.

Hebrews 12:1–2

Olympic hymn

97 LET US RUN WITH PERSEVERANCE

1 Let us run with perseverance
and on Jesus fix our eyes;
through the cross he came to glory,
faith's beginning and its prize.
Let us shed all things that hinder,
blur our vision, weigh us down;
look to him who brought redemption,
bore the cost and won the crown.

2 Some who run are counted heroes
gaining silver, bronze or gold;
all find joy in their competing,
round the track and round the world.
Some take part as paralympians,
climbing mountains to compete;
all need skill and strength and balance
for their lap to be complete.

3 Some will measure time or distance,
record speed or length or height;
all in squad or team or solo
know the rules to keep them right.
Some will not be there for medals;
they too share this world of sport,
all who coach, supply and steward –
vital champions in support.

4 Trained and tuned, let us be ready,
hear the signal, start the race,
focussed to complete the circuit
each in our appointed place.
Fully tested, still enduring,
on the goal we fix our eyes;
Christ for us has won the glory,
faith's beginning and its prize.

8787D   Tune: LUX EOI

Scriptures: 1 Cor 9:24–27   Phil 3:13-21   2 Tim 2:5; 4:7–8   Heb 12:1–2
Written: Bromley, Kent, 15–17 Jan 2012.
First published: *The Methodist Recorder*, 20 July 2012

This 'Olympic hymn' was suggested by Robert Draycott, the former chaplain of Eltham College who had already requested 3 hymns for the school—see *Walking by the River* (2008) nos.88–90. 'London 2012' was the big event for which the churches were preparing under the banner 'More than Gold', in which Robert had a share; this was written (appropriately?) at some speed, and had a more immediate impact than any other hymn I had written. It appeared on various websites and was sung at many services and related events that summer.

The Letter of James

When faith works

98   PURE JOY IS WHEN THROUGH MANY TRIALS

1   Pure joy is when through many trials
     God's children persevere;
     he promises the crown of life
     to those who love him here.

1:2–3, 12, 18

2   True faith will shine through lively deeds;
     without these, it is vain:
     God's word gives birth and vital growth,
     and firstfruits which remain.

2:17–18, 26   3:13, 17–18

3   Be wise in asking God for help,
     in setting doubts aside,
     and guarding hearts and hands and tongues
     from greed, revenge and pride.

1:5–6, 19   2:1   3:5–16   4:1–11   5:1–6

4   Lord God, you give us all we need
     of goodness and of grace;
     in Christ forgiving and forgiven
     we sing your glorious praise.

1:17   5:13–16

CM   Tune: SHOREHAM-BY-SEA by Christopher Hayward (1989),
or ST SAVIOUR

Scriptures: See notes to the stanzas; also 1 Kings 3:9–10   Prov 2:1–3   Matt 5:12   1 Cor 9:25
Gal 5:6   1 Pet 1:6
Written: Bromley, Kent, 23 Feb—11 March 2011
In February 2011, Helen Hayward of Penshurst Kent, widow of Christopher, suggested a need in her own
church (St John's Tunbridge Wells) for a hymn based on the letter of James. She hoped for a CM text which
could be sung to one of Chris's tunes. Towards the end of that month I sent her a draft, and after some
adjustments based on her suggestions, it was settled by 11th March and launched at St John's a little later;
then finally finalised (!), with help from Sara Thomson of Tonbridge, in April 2012.

James 3:18

Peace-receiving, peace-making

99   PEACE IS THE GIFT OF GOD'S TRUE REIGN

1   Peace is the gift of God's true reign,
of heaven come to earth;
of joy through travail, grief and pain,
the kingdom brought to birth.
> This is the hope the prophets saw
> through years of bitter strife;
> like us, they witnessed death and war
> but dared to dream of life.

2   Peace is the fruit the Spirit grows,
a harvest from above,
when justice like a river flows
with mercy, truth and love.
> This is the path we all must go,
> and walk afresh each day;
> there is no way to peace, we know:
> peace is itself the way.

3   Peace is the song from every land,
wherever we call home;
a word all nations understand:
eirene, pax, shalom.
> This is the goal for which we long,
> the purpose we make known,
> when we can march ten thousand strong
> or need to stand alone.

4   Peace is the power to get things done,
but not by spear or sword;
not pest or poison, bomb or gun,
but taking Christ as Lord.
> Peace is the name that Jesus bears,
> the Word, the Prince of peace;
> his title lasts through endless years,
> his love shall never cease.

5   Here is the gift of God's true reign,
the hope the prophets knew;
the Holy Spirit's fruit we gain,
the path we must pursue;
> here is the song we all can sing,
> the goal for which we aim,
> the power which God alone can bring,
> our peace in Jesus' name.

CMD   Tune: BROADCLYST by Sue Gilmurray (2016)

Scriptures: Ps 85:8–10; 122:6–9   Isa 2:1–5; 9:5–7   Mic 4:1–5; 5:4–5   Matt 26:50–52   Luke 2:13–14
Acts 10:36   Eph 2:14–18   Jas 3:18
Written: Herne Hill, SE London, January 2017
'Peace' in Scripture (*shalom, eirene*) is not only an absence of war between nations, nor only the forgiveness of our sins. This attempt to express some of its many facets came from an invitation from Sue Claydon of the Anglican Pacifist Fellowship, to mark its 80th birthday in 2017. Sue Gilmurray, who composed the music, also helped to shape the final form of what began as eight 4-line stanzas; the concluding one was her suggestion. Among those included here, the hymn was among the last to be written.

1 Peter 4:10–11

Creativity written, spoken, sung

100   FOR EVERY STORY, EVERY SONG

1   For every story, every song
which helps us know where we belong,
reminding us of ancient roots,
our birth and life, our growth and fruits:
      praise be to God the Giver!

2   For all who write and all who read
in pain or pleasure, wealth or need,
who edit, copy or translate
whatever is the name or date:
      praise be to God the Giver!

3   For those who sing and those who play,
compose, arrange, support and pray;
for special gifts, creative flair
not just for showing but to share:
      praise be to God the Giver!

4   For all those in the writing scene
of printed page or busy screen,
who work together or alone;
for scribes unsung, unnamed, unknown;
praise be to God the Giver!

5   For those who make the Scriptures clear,
who teach the mind by eye and ear;
who humble us, and clearly show
the way of Christ we need to go:
      praise be to God the Giver!

88887   new tune needed

Scriptures: Gen 4:19–21   Jer 36:4–8   Matt 23:34   1 Tim 4:13–16   1 Pet 4:10–11
Written: Bromley, Kent, started 2010, completed July 2012
In July 2012 I made time to tidy up and complete a clutch of half a dozen hymn texts I had begun to draft
some two years earlier; this was one of them. What first prompted it I cannot now recall, except that the
subject seems to be rarely prayed about in public, still less sung about. Time to change that? See also no.45.

1 Peter 4:12-17

God's suffering church

101   SPIRIT OF COMPASSION

1   Spirit of compassion,
in the time of trouble
look upon your people,
    save us from despair.
Set your seal upon us,
let your love indwell us;
your right hand uphold us;
    help us, hear our prayer.

2   Father of all mercies,
in our woes and wanderings
you will never leave us;
    you are our true home.
Through each hard oppression
keep our hope unconquered;
save us from destruction:
    may your Kingdom come.

3   Saviour, risen Master,
you have walked in weakness,
you have known the darkness,
    facing bitter night.
When our lives are broken
let your mercy heal us,
by your grace remake us,
    lead us into light.

4   Father, Son and Spirit,
Trinity eternal,
'Holy, Holy, Holy'
    is the church's song.
Maker, Saviour, Helper,
Source and Guide and Magnet,
yours be all the glory
    through the ages long!

6665D   new tune needed

Scriptures: Matt 6:10   John 13:30; 15:18–21; 16:33   Acts 14:22   2 Cor 1:3–4; 4:7–11; 6:3–10   2 Tim 3:10–12   Heb 13:5–6   1 Pet 4:12–17   Rev 4:8

Written: Herne Hill, SE London, 18–19 May 2016

This began as an approximate versification, in an unusual metre, of a prayer for persecuted churches, but it developed into a wider range of ideas.

1 Peter 5:1–4

Shepherds of God's flock

102 THE LORD CALLED MOSES WHEN HE WAS WITH THE SHEEP

1   The Lord called Moses
    when he was with the sheep,
    and set him over all
      the flock of God.
    May every leader
    who follows in his steps
    learn humbly as they walk
      the path he trod.

2   The Lord took David
    when he was with the sheep,
    and made him shepherd
      for a chosen race.
    May every pastor
    now called to tend the church
    enjoy a full supply of
      truth and grace.

3   The Lord chose Peter
    among the fishermen,
    gave him the task of feeding
      all the sheep.
    May every elder
    commissioned to that work
    be faithful in the charge
      he has to keep.

4   Our Saviour, Jesus,
    Chief Shepherd of your church,
    for us you gave your life,
      you laid it down;
    may we still follow
    and listen to your voice,
    and by your grace
      look forward to your crown.

5 6 10 D   new tune needed

Scriptures: Exod 3:1-10   Numb 12:3   1 Sam 16:1-13   Ps 77:20; 78:70-72   Isa 63:11   Mark 1:16-17
John 10:11-18; 21:15-17   Acts 20:28   1 Pet 5:1-4
Written: Herne Hill, SE London, 8–9 July 2015
This grew from thoughts on 1 Samuel 16 (the initial calling and anointing of David) during preparation for
a sermon on this chapter for Holy Redeemer Church, Streatham, S London.

1 Peter 5:10

God All-in-all

103   GOD OF ALL GRACE

1   God of all grace, you gave for us
your Son, the final Word:
his birth, his life, his work, his cross:
our raised, ascended Lord!

2   God of all truth, no cryptic view
is hidden from your eyes;
no theory, fact or find is new,
or takes you by surprise.

3   God of all hope, your mercies bless
the souls most deeply lost;
none need be left in hopelessness
for you have met its cost.

4   God of all love, which brightly burns
to make our hearts your home;
your Spirit leads till Christ returns,
and untold glories come.

5   All grace, all truth, all hope, all love:
God, at your feet we fall!
Through earth and hell and heaven above
you reign, the All-in-all.

CM   Tune: NUN DANKET ALL or DUNFERMLINE

Scriptures: Ps 33:13–15   John 1:14   Rom 15:13   1 Cor 15:28   Eph 3:16–19   Heb 1:1–2; 4:13
1 Pet 5:10

Written: Herne Hill, SE London, June 2016

'The God of all grace' was a phrase from one of the Sunday readings (1 Peter 5:10) on 12th June 2016 at
St Paul's, Herne Hill. It gave me food for thought, and for further writing, during the week that followed.

2 Peter 3:9

The patience of God

104 THE NAME OF THE LORD REVEALED FROM ABOVE

1 The name of the LORD
   revealed from above
   is patient and kind,
   unsparing in love;
   compassionate, faithful
   for all who believe,
   so slow to be angry,
   so swift to forgive!

2 So patient was God
   before the great flood,
   withholding his wrath
   he planned for our good.
   With Moses his servant
   God spoke face to face,
   displaying his patience
   in judgement and grace.

3 So patient was Christ
   with all who came near,
   so patient to teach
   those willing to hear;
   so patient in suffering,
   so patient in death
   when for our redemption
   he spent his last breath.

4 The promise is sure:
   the Lord will return,
   this earth be destroyed,
   the elements burn;
   but God in his patience
   prolonging his call
   gives time for repentance,
   shows mercy to all.

5 This patience of God
   how glorious to see –
   so patient with all,
   so patient with me!
   Because to such rebels
   such patience is shown,
   we love and adore him
   who makes us his own.

5555 6565   Tune: HANOVER

Scriptures: v.1: Exod 34:5–6   Num 14:18–19   Ps 86:15
v.2: Gen 6:7–8   1 Pet 3:20   Exod 32:14; 33:11
v.3: Mark 4:1–2; 6:32–34   Luke 15:1   1 Pet 2:23–24   Heb 12:2–3   Eph 1:7
v.4: 2 Pet 3:9–12   Rom 2:4   1 Tim 2:4
v.5: 1 Tim 1:15–16   Rom 9:22–26
Written: Bromley, Kent, 25–26 January 2013
David Hircock, Pastor of Hayes Lane Baptist Church, Bromley, asked for suggestions for songs on God's patience, relating to 2 Peter 3:9. To our surprise we found none; so I wrote this in unusual haste between Friday evening and Saturday, ready for Sunday when it was sung at the church, with Jonathan Gooch at the keyboard.

2 Peter 3:13

Creation made, spoiled, renewed

105   FINE WEAVER OF ALL THINGS, OUR GOD

1   Fine weaver of all things, our God:
you thread all earth's beauty and form,
your fingers sustaining our world,
the sunshine, the cloud and the storm.
Skilled architect, building in stone,
wise planter of everything green,
the red of the blood, the white bone,
the rhythm of heartbeats unseen.

2   Good farmer of soil and of seed,
first gardener of colour and scent,
of harvests supplying our need,
the fruit of the land we are lent.
Your sands are for many their home,
who look to the sky for the rain;
your forests where myriads roam,
and travelling flocks of the plain.

3   Prime source of each river and stream,
rich Lord of the deep and the dark,
the dancing of dolphins, the gleam
of the salmon, the seal and the shark.
And now we explore distant skies,
discoveries stretching the mind,
as science brings shock or surprise
and wonder at what we shall find.

4   Yet such sore pollution we see,
the spoiling of nature displayed,
humanity no longer free;
how far from the peace which you made!
What rebels we all have become,
what wasters and wreckers of good;
our minds and our consciences numb,
our hearts which have not understood.

5   Have mercy, Lord! This is your earth,
we cry in our weakness to you;
your promise gives hope of rebirth,
in Christ all creation made new.
Till then let us care for this place,
in wisdom your riches to use,
to treasure these moments of grace,
as stewards of faith and good news

8888D anapaestic   Tune; TREWEN, or new tune needed

Scriptures: Gen 1; 3:17–19   Ps 8:3, 6–8; 65:9–13; 104:10–25; 139:13–16   Matt 19:28   Rom 8:20–23
2 Pet 3:13   Rev 21:5
Written: Herne Hill, SE London, May–June 2016
The first two lines grew from an early draft of a different hymn, and suggested other possible ways of exploring the theme of God as both Creator and Rescuer.

1 John 4:7–16
Show the world what God is like

106   TO SHOW THE WORLD THAT GOD IS REAL

1 To show the world that God is real
what binding duty, boundless joy!
His Spirit will inspire our zeal
to search so deep, to aim so high!

2 To show the world that God is great:
a heavenly task for earth below!
To care, to rule, to re-create,
such wisdom and such works to show.

3 To show the world that God is good:
his ways are right; his words are true;
and when that truth is understood
we find his mercies ever new.

4 To show the world that God is just
whatever fears and doubts may rise;
what stumbling witness, dawning trust
in humble minds and opened eyes.

5 To show the world that God is near
though often seeming far away;
the Holy Spirit still makes clear
and prompts dull hearts to praise and pray.

6 To show the world that God is love
by lip and life, by word and deed;
the cross of Christ alone can prove
how vast his grace, how deep our need!

7 Praise God, so great, so good, so fair,
so close to those who learn by grace
to find his glory everywhere,
his love which shines in every place!

LM: Tune FESTUS or DEUS TUORUM MILITUM

Scriptures: Ps 48:1; 99:2; 100; 145   Lam 3:22–23   Acts 17:27–28   Jas 1:17
1 Pet 2:9   1 John 4:7–16
Written: Bromley, Kent, March and May 2013; Herne Hill, SE London, July 2015.
It was the first line of what is now my third stanza which struck me from a sermon by David Hircock (Hayes Lane Baptist Church, Bromley), and which was the starting-point for this text which grew both backwards and forwards. I attended HLBC from 2009 to 2013; the sermon, one of a series on the Letter of James, was on Jas 1:17, and the hymn was drafted sporadically in 2013 and finalised two years later. We are still trying to show these things, but the world is slow to respond; indeed without the Holy Spirit it cannot, and neither can we.

2 John

Words for the chosen lady and her children

107   THE TRUTH WHICH LIVES IN US BY GRACE

1   The truth which lives in us by grace,
    by grace is ours for ever,
    truth from the Father and the Son,
    one God, the true Life-giver.

2   And grace, the perfect twin of truth,
    in Jesus' incarnation,
    is that free gift which comes by faith
    and heralds our salvation.

3   And as his mercy fills our hearts
    and overflows in blessing,
    so we are cleansed, our sins forgiven,
    and live, one Lord confessing.

4   The costly peace which Jesus won
    by this world is not given;
    yet peace from God can bring on earth
    the ways and works of heaven.

5   The teaching we have heard from God
    rings true for all believers;
    it keeps us constant on the path
    and guards against deceivers.

6   And when God's children walk in truth
    with joy this news is greeted;
    but meeting, talking, face to face,
    we find that joy completed.

7   And love, the old and new command
    for neighbour, sister, brother:
    as God in Christ has first loved us
    so we love one another.

8787 iambic   Tune: THE FOLLOWERS

Scriptures: Mark 12:28–34   John 8:31–32; 10:4–5; 13:34; 14:27; 15:12,17
1 John 3:23; 4:7–12,19   2 John   3 John 4
Written: Herne Hill, SE London, 1–2 Nov 2015.
This was written shortly after no.108, qv, as I thought that 2 John might also be expressed in the form of a hymn. But the approach is different; this time the text is based on seven of what seem to be key words in this brief Epistle, addressed to 'the chosen lady [the church?] and her children'. It also draws on other basic material in the Gospel according to John.

3 John

Short metre for a short letter

108   WHAT JOY, WHEN ALL THE TALK

1   What joy, when all the talk
     is how things prosper well;
     and when believers love to walk
     in truth, with news to tell:

2   When even strangers find
     a welcome on their ways;
     a church hospitable and kind,
     a home of thankful praise:

3   When those who once went out
     to serve the one true Name
     see faith replacing fear and doubt,
     forgiveness drowning shame.

4   And where this high ideal
     seems harder to maintain,
     Lord God, when we go wrong or fail
     revive our health again!

5   Hold us to what is good,
     and bless our friends with peace;
     your word be taught and understood,
     your mercies never cease.

Praise Trust   SM Tune: PURE IN HEART by Christopher Norton (1999);
or VENICE

Scriptures: Rom 12:9–12   Heb 13:1–2   2 John 4   3 John
Written: Herne Hill, SE London, 1–2 October 2015
In September 2015 Jim Ransome (of Stanway, Essex) pointed out that no hymn based on the 3rd Letter of John appeared in any index he knew. My own checking confirmed this gap, which suggested a call to action, from a punchy Scripture highly relevant to our 21st-century churches. Although many of our greatest writers have given us Short Metre hymns, more recently this simple pattern of 6686 has fallen into neglect or even discredit. But it seemed eminently suitable to partner a short Epistle.

Revelation 3:18
That we may see

109   IF WE KNEW WHERE TO LOOK

1   If we knew where to look, we'd see the lights
   across the city roofs or darkened fields;
   our inward gaze can miss so many sights
   which only outward, upward vision yields.

2   If we knew where to look, we'd see the stars,
   the planets, comets, moons and galaxies;
   beyond by far our Mercury or Mars,
   and distant patterns dwarfing such as these.

3   If we knew where to look, we'd see the specks
   of plants and creatures underneath our feet;
   creation's billion marvels, tiny flecks
   of secret beauty, in themselves complete.

4   If we knew where to look, we'd see the truth
   for mind and heart, the treasures in God's book,
   with power to bring us light, in age or youth,
   and rescue us, if we knew where to look.

5   If we knew where to look, we'd see the Lord,
   Creator, Saviour, from the Spirit shown;
   by many still denied or long ignored,
   but in his grace believed and loved and known.

10 10 10 10   Tune: FARLEY CASTLE

Scriptures: Mark 8:18; 10:51–52   John 1:9–18; 9:25   Rev 3:18
Written: Herne Hill, SE London, 22–23 Dec 2016.
Even from the train it can be important to know where to look for a recognisable tower or spire, castle or cathedral—for example, travelling home through Penge East just before Christmas 2016 and spotting some floodlights, where this idea began to take shape. And there are far more vital directions in which to look, to see 'the everlasting Light'. This was among the final hymns I wrote before closing the list in preparation for this present book; but see also *Joy in the City* by Marjorie Idle (Kingsway, 1988, 1995), chapter one.

Revelation 18:1

Christ's glory, earth's brightness

110 THE EARTH IS MADE BRIGHT WITH THE GLORY

1 The earth is made bright with the glory
of angels appearing on high;
the shepherds are stunned by the greeting,
their presence transforming the sky.
The earth is made bright with the glory
of Jesus, the world-changing light;
the ears that were blocked up, he opens,
and blind eyes are given their sight.

2 The earth is made bright with his glory
through darkness, desertion and loss;
believers are touched by the wonder,
the reign of the Lord from his cross.
The earth is made bright with his glory
that morning which none had foreseen,
the grave in the garden stands open;
he shines where the shadows have been.

3 The earth will be bright with his glory,
beyond all our skill to express:
creation made new, as he promised
to judge, to redeem and to bless.
The earth is made bright with his glory
wherever his story is heard;
let us be alight with his Spirit,
our world be reclaimed by the Word.

9898D anapaestic Tune; CRUGYBAR or YR HEN DDARBI (OLD DERBY);
or new tune

Scriptures: Ps 96:13 Isa 35:5 Matt 5:14–16; 11:4–5; 24:27–30; 25:31–33 Mark 15:33,39 Luke 2:8–14; 21:27–28; 23:39–44 John 1:5,9,14; 20:1–16 Rom 8:23 2 Cor 4:3–6 1 Pet 2:9 2 Pet 3:13 Rev 18:1
Written: Herne Hill, SE London, 17–18 June 2016
A single phrase from my daily reading struck me forcibly in June 2016: '…and the earth was made bright with his glory': Revelation 18:1 (ESV). And this was only a single angel, in an otherwise dark context! So it struck me that these words had many other biblical resonances, too many indeed to list; but here are a few. They also refute Swinburne's notorious lines about the 'pale Galilean' whose breath turns the world grey. Billions have found it otherwise.

Revelation 22:13 (one)
Alpha and Omega—1

111   ADVOCATE, AMEN, ANOINTED

1 Advocate, Amen, Anointed,
Brightness joining earth and sky;
Christ our Centre, Crown and Captain,
Dawn and Dayspring from on high:
End, Emmanuel, Eternal,
Firstborn and Foundation-stone;
Gift and Glory, Guide and Guardian,
Heart's Desire, our Hope alone.

2 Intercessor, truest Image,
Joy and Judge of all our race;
King of kings and Key to freedom,
Lamb of God and Lord of grace.
Mary's Son, Messiah, Manna,
saving Name, the Nazarene;
Only Son and perfect Offering,
Prince, and Priest who makes us clean.

3 Radiance, Reward, Redeemer,
Servant, Star and shining Sun;
Teacher, Treasure, Truth and Tower,
Urgent, Unexpected one:
Virgin-born, true Vine and Vision
Wedding-guest and Wisdom's skill;
Yes to every pledge and promise,
Zeal to do your Father's will.

4 But what titles can contain you,
far beyond all words we use?
Great I AM, transcendent, holy,
yet you speak, to bring good news!
Hallelujah! For Christ Jesus
let our richest songs outpour:
Alpha, Omega, we praise you,
First and Last for evermore.

8787D   Tune: ALLELUIA

Scriptures: Rev 22:16, and others too many to list
Written: Herne Hill, SE London, 24-26 January 2016
Some distinguished writers have structured hymns on the various names and titles used in Scripture of God or of the Lord Jesus Christ. But I have not found any who adopt the plan of using one initial letter per line. Psalms such as 25 or 119 show that such verbal patterns (in the original language or in paraphrase) need not hinder their congregational or devotional use. This hymn is a twin of no.112, 'All-in-all, our full Atonement'; having drafted a much longer text, I wrote these as more manageable offshoots of that.

Revelation 22:13 (two)
Alpha and Omega—2

112 ALL-IN-ALL, OUR FULL ATONEMENT

1 All-in-all, our full Atonement,
Bridegroom, Brother, burning bright;
Counsellor, our Calm, our Comfort,
Christ our Door and our Delight.
Everlasting, ever-loving,
Fountain, Fulness, faithful Friend;
Guarantor and Guest and Giver,
Heir of heaven without end.

2 Once an Infant, newborn Israel,
Jesus, justice in your hand;
Kingdom of the poor, and Kindness,
Life and Light for every land:
Master, Mighty God and Mystery,
Newness, now the nations' Lord;
Outcast once, the One unrivalled,
Price once paid, our Peace restored.

3 Refugee and Resurrection,
Seed and Shelter, Song and Son,
Testimony, Teacher, Traveller,
Unstained but Uplifted one;
Victim for a time, then Victor,
living Water, Way and Word;
Yesterday, today, for ever,
Zion's one unchanging Lord.

4 But what titles can contain you,
far beyond all words we use?
Great I AM, transcendent, holy,
yet you speak, to bring good news!
Hallelujah! For Christ Jesus
let our richest songs outpour:
Alpha, Omega, we praise you,
First and Last for evermore.

8787D Tune: ALLELUIA

Scriptures: Rev 22:13, and others too many to list
Written: Herne Hill , SE London, 24-26 Jan 2016
See the notes to no.111, 'Amen, Advocate, Anointed'.

LOCAL AND
SPECIAL

Stepney Greencoat School, Limehouse, London E14

113 STEPNEY GREENCOAT, SING THIS SONG

1 Stepney Greencoat, sing this song,
   this is where we all belong,
   trusting God who makes us strong:
   we are Stepney Greencoat!
      Lots of laughs and sometimes tears,
      faith and love can beat our fears;
      we've been here 300 years!
   Thank you, God our Father.

Chorus:
Stepney Greencoat, come and see;
all together we agree,
this is just the place to be –
Thank you, God our Father!

2 Stepney Greencoat is our name;
   things may change or stay the same:
   what a special day we came
   here to Stepney Greencoat!
      Jesus can make all things new,
      gave himself for me and you;
      shows us what we all can do,
   Thank you, God our Father!

Chorus:
Stepney Greencoat, come and see…

3 Friends and families, teachers all,
   cooks and cleaners, short and tall,
   workers, helpers, big and small,
   we are Stepney Greencoat!
      Let us show you what we mean:
      we've been here since Anne was Queen,
      proud of London E14 –
   Thank you, God our Father!

Chorus:
Stepney Greencoat, come and see…

Tune: BOBBY SHAFTOE with chorus (2nd half of tune) repeated.

Scriptures: 2 Cor 5:17   Gal 2:20   Eph 5:19–20   2 Tim 2:1   Col 3:15–17   Rev 21:5
Written: Bromley, Kent: first draft, summer 2009; final text 26 March 2010.
Stepney Greencoat CofE Primary School in the parish of Limehouse, E London, celebrated its tercente-
nary in 2010. As I had been a school parent, chair of governors, taker of assemblies etc, during my time
as Rector (1976–89), I was delighted to be asked to write a song to mark the occasion. After various drafts
this was the agreed version, duly sung at the special celebrations in June and July.

Church of the Holy Redeemer, Streatham, London SW16

114   EIGHTY YEARS OF TRUSTING JESUS

1   Eighty years of trusting Jesus
    great Redeemer, holy One:
    fourscore, like the years of Moses
    when his work had just begun:
        every week a new beginning,
        every day a race to run.

2   Eighty years of loving Jesus;
    Lord whose love remains the same,
    sent to suffer and to triumph
    in the world to which he came:
        towns of Britain, towers of London,
        streets of Streatham, love his name!

3   Eighty years of serving Jesus,
    thanks for all who've gone before;
    building for the ones who follow,
    we too make our calling sure
        sharing news of sins forgiven,
        peace with God for evermore!

4   Eighty years of praising Jesus:
    every language, join to pray;
    come for mending and re-making –
    none who comes is turned away:
        Hallelujah! In one Spirit
        praise the Lord with us today!

878787   Tune: REGENT SQUARE

Scriptures: Exod 7:7   Ps 90:10   Rom 5:1   1 Cor 9:24–27   Heb 12:1
Written: Bromley, Kent, 21–23 July 2011
For the 80th Birthday in 2012 of the Church of the Holy Redeemer, Streatham, London SW16. Having
already written one for their 75th anniversary (see 'When Abraham at seventy-five', no.100 in *Walking by
the River*), I was asked by the vicar Ian Gilmour and his wife Denise to provide something similar five years
on. I wasn't sure what kind of music they had in mind; the tune named here was Denise's suggestion. This
at least gave me the metre, while Moses took over from Abraham in providing the basis for a theme. For
more general use it would need considerable adaptation.

Eltham College, London SE 9

115 BLACKHEATH TO MOTTINGHAM, WALKING THE MILES

1 Blackheath to Mottingham, walking the miles,
Old Barn to Mansion, by streams, over stiles;
smoke from the railway to sun on the trees –
that new generation faced changes like these.

2 One hundred years have gone by since that
  day,
thousands of memories passed on their way;
as we remember, give honour to all
the parents and families heeding God's call.

3 So many names are enrolled on our boards,
rows of grey photos, bright cups and rewards;
some are forgotten and gone to their rest
but not before faithfully giving their best.

4 Many were challenged to travel the earth,
moved by God's Spirit, the spring of new birth;
learning and teaching and sharing his grace,
enduring with Christ and completing their
  race.

5 On goes the story, the torch in our hands;
God's love has space for all-comers, all lands:
age of the internet, yet still the same
one need in our world, and our hope in one Name.

10 10 10 11   Tune: SLANE

Scriptures: Matt 12:21   John 3:5–8   Rom 1:11–12; 16:25–27   Heb 12:1–2   1 Cor 9:24–25

Written: Bromley, Kent, November 2011; revised January 2012

First published: *Eltham College Hymn Book*, Gresham Books 2016

Another Eltham College Hymn (see *Walking by the River*, 2008, nos.87–90), as requested in November 2011 by another Chaplain, Peter Swaffield. The 'School for the Sons of Missionaries', as it then was, moved from 'The Old Barn' at Blackheath to what had been the naval college at Mottingham, on 30 January 1912. The centenary was due to be celebrated in style; Peter suggested that yet another new hymn might be useful. From 3 or 4 tunes which he proposed and two drafts which I offered, we eventually agreed on this text to SLANE. After further work in response to comments from Peter, Alistair Tighe (Music Director) and Paul Henderson (Headmaster) by Jan 12th I had done all I could, and on the actual anniversary (30th) it featured in three similar chapel services for the school's three age-groups, each one introduced with a warm welcome from the Headmaster and a challenging gospel address by the Chaplain. Each also featured some fine music from organ, brass section and school choir; the junior school, of course, sang with the most enthusiasm. I found it all very moving; reflecting on my text some hours later, I wondered if it was rather idealistic. But if you can't express ideals in chapel...?

Cambewarra Union Church, New South Wales, Australia

116 GLORY TO GOD, WHO HAS BLESSED US

1 Glory to God, who has blessed us
　　from humble beginnings!
He alone judges or praises our losses
　　and winnings.
　　We count the years,
landmarks of laughter or tears,
building this marathon innings.

2* Praise to the Son of Man, gracing
　　the home of Zacchaeus,
seeking and saving the lost, on his
　　mission to free us!
　　Saints in the past
aimed for the targets that last:
how will our grandchildren see us?

3 Glory to Jesus, who makes us his
　　newborn creation,
dying and rising, one hope for our
　　world and our nation!
　　In him we live;
countless the reasons to give
thanks for today's celebration.

4* Here among mountain and farm, by
　　the trees and the river,
we come to pray, and to praise our
　　Creator and Giver;
　　saved from the fire
making his will our desire,
knowing his love is for ever.

5 Praise to the Spirit, who binds all
　　believers in union;
one in the Word, and his table of
　　richest communion!
　　Here we are given
foretastes of new earth and heaven,
promise of joyful reunion.

6 Glory to God, Holy Trinity, Source
　　of all blessing,
Spring of our worship and witness,
　　one faith all confessing!
　　What lies ahead?
Growing by all God has said;
glories beyond human guessing.

14 14 4 7 8　　Tune: LOBE DEN HERREN

Scriptures: Luke 19:1–10　　Rom 11:36　　1 Cor 8:6; 12:4–6　　Heb 5:9; 9:12　　Rev 21:1
Written: Bromley, Kent, 9–11 March 2016
A 150th anniversary hymn, as requested by my old friend Robert Emery, known since schooldays in 1943, for Cambewarra Union (village) Church, NSW, opened 29 April 1866. The asterisked verses may be omitted, as being of purely local interest; the beginning of the church and its first building are traced back to Zaccheus [sic] Bice, one of three founding trustees, and in 1877 the building narrowly escaped destruction by fire.

St Peter's College, Oxford

117   OUR ROCK AND OUR CASTLE, IN GOD WE ARE STRONG

1 Our Rock and our Castle, in God we are
        strong,
    and with Christ's apostle we learn to
        belong:
    as from Simon Peter is chosen the
        name,
    we joyfully feature his title and fame.

2 He knew about fishing, and feeding the
        flock,
    and eating and washing, and building
        on rock;
    the cross is our symbol; the cockerel
        and keys
    are signs to be humble for days such as
        these.

3 They once called him simple, untrained
        in the schools,
    but soon in God's temple he learned to
        break rules
    where, filled with the Spirit, he spoke of
        God's grace,
    so we can inherit his work in this place.

4 So praise for the best of St Peter's good
        news
    for east and for west, as for Gentiles and
        Jews;
    his message for all peoples, home and
        abroad:
    our hope is to call on the name of the
        Lord.

11 11 11 11   Tune: MONTGOMERY

Scriptures: Incidents from the life and work of the apostle Peter, including Matt 4,16, and 26   Luke 5
John 13, 21   Acts 2, 4, 10–12   1 Pet 5
Written: Herne Hill, SE London, Nov–Dec 2016
Unlike some of these localised texts, this one may be usable in other places—namely, those adopting the
name of 'St Peter' in their title; St Peter's Church, Palgrave (Suffolk) springs to mind. But it was written in
appreciation of my three years at St Peter's Oxford (formerly 'Pot Hall'). I added three verses made specific
to my old college by naming some revered names from its history, but agreed with my contemporary John
Wesson that this did not really work. I still have them on file as a sample of affectionate lighter verse.

APPENDIX:
SOME EXTRAS

1 Timothy2:1–6
For monarchs, and why

A: GOD SAVE OUR GRACIOUS QUEEN,
GOD BLESS AND GUARD OUR QUEEN

1   God save our gracious Queen,
    God bless and guard our Queen,
      long live the Queen!
    Guard us in liberty,
    bless us with unity,
    save us from tyranny:
      God save the Queen!

2   Lord be our nation's light,
    guide us in truth and right:
      in you we stand;
    give us your faithfulness,
    keep us from selfishness,
    raise us to godliness:
      God save our land!

3   Spirit of love and life,
    healing our nation's strife,
      on you we call:
    teach us your better way,
    grant us your peace today;
    God bless our Queen, we pray,
      God save us all!

664 6664   Tune: NATIONAL ANTHEM

Scriptures: 1 Sam 10:24 Isa 42:6 Rom 8:2;13:1–5 1 Cor 12:31 1 Tim 2:1–5 1 Pet 2:13–17
Written: Peckham, SE London, 1980.
First published: *Hymns for Today's Church*, Hodder and Stoughton1982

Unlike others in the book, this text was written and published over 35 years ago. It produced a small media frenzy in August 1982 owing to a pre-publication leak by John Capon in the *Sunday Telegraph*. Headlines, articles, letters, interviews and (best of all) cartoons proliferated until more vital issues reclaimed the main news. At the time, the words-committee for HTC agreed to own (and copyright) this version, but now with the agreement of the few surviving members, its authorship can be acknowledged.

This hymn-book also included what it called the 'traditional version', though its textual history is more complicated and colourful than that suggests; see among other sources two books called *God Save The Queen*, by Percy Scholes (1954) and Ian Bradley (2012).

As to the content of this approach, it can be seen as Christian, Trinitarian and patriotic, while being more applicable to a constitutional monarchy; its place now may be simply a 20th-century footnote, from one who as a teenager was present in central London on Coronation Day, 2nd June 1953.

B: TEXTS FOR AN ANTHEM

Part 1:

If the Spirit of God is alive in you,
you can set your hearts on what pleases him:
  Christ, revive us and all your people today.

If the Spirit of Christ is at work in you,
with your body and mind you can serve in his world:
  Christ, refresh us and all your people today.

If the Spirit of love is poured out in you,
With a thankful hope you can trust his word:
  Christ, renew us and all your people today.

Part 2:

Welcome one another, as Christ has welcomed you!
Here are new openings; let us all be ready.
  May your Holy Spirit, Lord, train us for God's calling.

Love one another, as Christ has first loved you!
Such opportunities; let us take them gladly.
  May your Holy Spirit, Lord, shape us for God's glory.

Serve one another, as Christ was servant too!
This is our offering; soul and body's worship.
  May your Holy Spirit, Lord, fit us for God's moment.

Part 3:

You are God's temple, his Spirit lives in you;
bought with a price and called to be holy:
    Lord Jesus, employ us in renewed commitment.

You are Christ's body, his likeness formed in you;
raised from the dead, equipped for his purpose:
    Lord Jesus, empower us in renewed commitment.

You are God's garden, his fruit will grow in you;
filled with his gifts, created for sharing:
    Lord Jesus, enrich us in renewed commitment.

These verses, based on several New Testament texts, were written in August 2009 for a Methodist Church in Kent, in response to an urgent request to help celebrate a new beginning for the congregation. The three parts were options from which others could choose. In the event, no music was composed for them and they were not needed, but they remain on file for others to explore.

A hymn for peace

C: IF PEACE REMAINS OUR PURPOSE

1 If peace remains our purpose
   what wisdom we shall need
   to meet a world so broken
   with healing word and deed!
      We dare not claim the high ground;
      we all need truth and grace
      to humble our pretensions
      and find a servant's place.

2 With new and fearsome evils
   in every shifting scene,
   we feel dismayed and tarnished
   and no-one's hands are clean.
      The lies that would deceive us
      divide us as we pray;
      yet still we cry for answers
      to blow the fog away.

3 Where all is pain and darkness
   and certainties are rare,
   our one unfailing watchword
   shall be, 'The Lord is here!'
      For in our seeming chaos
      he has not lost control,
      nor yet withdrawn his presence
      nor moved the Kingdom's goal.

4 For Jesus says, 'Be perfect,
   and raise your eyes above';
   our Father is our pattern
   for justice and for love.
      If we love God, each other,
      and neighbours far and near,
      no enemy shall goad us
      to hatred or to fear.

5 Yes, peace is still our purpose,
   non-violence our creed,
   and costly love, the programme
   that meets all human need.
      Come, Holy Spirit, guide us!
      The empty cross still stands,
      and Christ in risen glory
      the hope of all the lands.

7676D Tune: PINHOE by Sue Gilmurray

Scriptures: Scriptures: Ps 34:14   Ezek 48:35   Zech 2:10   Matt 5:43–48; 26:52; 27:34–40   Luke 21:28
John 15:9–12
Written: Herne Hill, SE London, 14–16 Jan 2017
A follow-up to no.99.

Another, from the Old Testament histories

D: DO NOT GO UP TO FIGHT AGAINST YOUR BROTHERS

1 'Do not go up to fight against your
   brothers!'
   The Lord who gave this negative decree
   gives positive commands to love our
   neighbours,
   which set them and ourselves most
   truly free.

2 So if we fly up high to bomb our
   brothers
   and afterwards add up our score of hits,
   we won't forget to count the children,
   mothers,
   and unknown sisters we have smashed
   to bits.

3 Or if we are not there, and do not see it
   but on the news, when it is granted
   space,
   we shudder, switch it off, and then
   agree it
   is not our fault some deaths are hard
   to face.

4 But though we kill our neighbours and
   our brothers,
   not they nor we shall pay the final
   price:
   in every murder it is God who suffers;
   Christ hangs again, a blood-marked
   sacrifice.

11 10 11 10 Tune: HIGHWOOD

Scriptures: 1 Kings 12:24 (= 2 Chronicles 11:4).
Written: Bromley, Kent, 2012.
An ancient yet modern warning? People of the tribe of Judah are warned not to attack their fellow-Hebrews—in spite of presumed serious provocation.

For a revered and beloved hymnwriter

E: WHAT SEEK WE...?

What seek we in the hymns of TDS?
Precision rhyming, rhythm, metre, stress,
good sense and Scripture content? Answer: Yes!

Earth's need and heaven's beauty here displayed;
our free salvation, and the price once paid
by One now risen—Christ, in light arrayed!

From homes and holidays, what wealth outpoured!
Blackheath and Bramerton, Ruan Minor, Ford:
let each much-loved location praise the Lord!

Green Sevenoaks, and travels on the train
bring leaves and lines to greet the Saviour's reign;
soon comes a card: true Christmas dawns again!

Can it be ninety years? Rich fruit is here
in texts that challenge, teach, inspire and cheer;
unnumbered blessings through each numbered year!

Dear Timothy, how privileged your friends,
as crafted verse with soaring music blends,
to share and sing the Life that never ends:

Alleluia!

Written: Herne Hill, SE London, November 2016.
Timothy Dudley-Smith, retired Bishop and acknowledged prince among contemporary hymnwriters, celebrated his ninetieth birthday (a month early, for logistical reasons) in Advent (November) 2016. I was not the only one to break into verse for this happy choral and gospel event, but Timothy has kindly allowed me to reprint my own tribute here. The five place-names comprise most of the 'homes and holidays' where his hymn-texts were written; see his own collections *A House of Praise*, vols 1 and 2 (OUP, 2003 and 2015).

Not a hymn; but thanks for writers and writings.

F: IN EVERY TREASURED BOOK

The year 2016 was rich in commemoration of the four centuries since the death of William Shakespeare. I wondered if there was material here for a hymn; my friend and exact contemporary David Mowbray has skilfully woven biblical and post-biblical figures into the praise of God. I found that difficult, but also wondered if some verses might stretch far wider than Shakespeare; where are the hymns of gratitude for creative writing of all kinds? This not-quite-a-hymn is the result. If it doesn't quite work, or falls between too many stools, others may like to take up the challenge.

Some may reckon that Chaucer, Donne, Wordsworth, Keats, Tennyson or Dickens should be included; I might have added Cranmer, Blake, Cobbold, Murray (James), Owen, Brittain, Woolf, Sayers, Peake, Solzhenitsyn, Shute, Thomas (RS), Nicholson (N), Wodehouse, Milligan or Dudley-Smith. But there are limits even when we are not actually singing; and these lines feature at least some of my own favourite authors. They took this final shape in May 2016.

In every treasured book
their words span depth and height;
from Caedmon's song and Langland's folk
to Spenser's sweet delight.
And who can match the bard
of Stratford and the Globe,
whose pen is sharper than a sword,
a prince without a robe?

But can fair Paradise
be structured to a plan?
How grandly Milton justifies
the ways of God to man!
While Herbert's skill displays
his church in patterned rhyme,
to serve his Lord in tuneful praise:
so rich, so short a time!

Pilgrims not only dream
if Bunyan is their guide,
but find the gate, the track, the stream
and gain the farther side.
Great Johnson, born to teach,
in talk and toil most rare,
gives meanings to define our speech,
with piety and prayer.

Wesley and Watts remain
when words and music join,
wherever Christ is known to reign,
and lavish love divine.
The grace that bids us meet,
like Newton, learn to pray,
makes his and Cowper's hymns complete
for this and every day.

The Brontë sisters' care,
Austen's and Eliot's art,
in drawing human character
can move the dullest heart.
Two learned Oxford dons
give trees and trolls a tongue;
the lion roars, the king returns,
the weak subvert the strong.

And thousands down the years,
prizewinners or 'anon',
give us such wonder, laughter, tears,
and still their craft goes on.
For all whose writing lifts
our spirits through the page,
praise God who brings such treasured gifts
from each succeeding age!

G: Two poems (from many) for Marjorie

Daring to follow the example of wordsmiths Thomas Troeger and Andrew Hawes, in including a final tribute to Marjorie Grace, for nearly forty years my wife and fellow-writer. Here are two of many verses written between 2003 and the present. Marjorie's grave is in Oakley churchyard, Suffolk; the inscription on the headstone begins: 'Remember Jesus Christ, risen from the dead'; 2 Timothy 2:8.

WRITTEN AND ENGRAVED

A scribbled note, a shopping list,
a name in biro on the wrist,
a number on an envelope,
a message pad of haste, or hope:
such scripts may carry hidden power
but often die within the hour.

A letter or a poem, then,
using a silver-shining pen
or now appearing on the screen
and run off on our new machine:
a little longer these may last,
until a week, a year, has passed.

But the best text I ever wrote
and learned by heart, to keep and quote,
exposed to wind and rain and sun
and read by many, few or none,
may last a century or two
as it grows old, yet ever new.

So every word must carry weight,
the spelling right, the layout straight,
fine-carved on smooth and solid stone;
among my works it stands alone.
I wrote it, and it writes to me
of my beloved Marjorie.

London, Oakley and Bromley, September 2005

TO EVERYTHING THERE IS A SEASON

'Grow old along with me'?
But that was not to be;
we scarcely reached beyond our middle-ageing.
When you were snatched away
and dark replaced the day,
we lost the unsought battle we were waging.

You never saw that Spring,
so early you took wing
from home and hospice on your flight to glory.
Yet those who caught your smile
even for that little while
were glad to have some share in your tough story.

The snowdrops bloomed for you
in February dew,
the day we bore your coffin through the grasses.
We laid your body where
the trees were tall and bare;
yet even then we knew that Winter passes.

And now I go that way
by train, sometimes to stay
close to your body's temporary prison.
But you are not alone,
and flowers adorn the stone
which shows that you, with Jesus Christ, are risen.

Bromley, August 2012

While it doesn't affect the significance of these hymns either way, I have enjoyed writing the majority of my total output (before 2018) in three homes of historic and literary interest.

In Poplar (1971-76), St Matthias' Vicarage was where the poet and translator Samuel Hoole (1757-1839) once lived; incumbent for 36 years until his death, as a young clergyman he was a close friend of Dr Samuel Johnson. A slightly earlier resident was another East India Company Chaplain Gloster Ridley (1702-1774), a translator whose other great interest was the stage, and who for some years lived 'mainly' in Poplar and was buried there.

At Limehouse (1976-89), the present Rectory was built on the site of the house where Charles Dickens (1812-1870) used to stay; he wrote *Hard Times* and other books while visiting his nephew and godson, the sailmaker and chandler Christopher Huffam, in Church Row, later renamed Newell Street. The best-selling novelist Florence Barclay (1862-1921), daughter of the 1870s Rector Samuel Charlesworth, lived in the earlier Rectory a few yards away across the Limehouse Cut, but her published writing dates from after her marriage.

Then a predecessor of mine **at Oakley** (1989-95) was the Puritan preacher and Bible-commentator William Greenhill (1591[or '98?]-1671); his parsonage stood on the north side of the churchyard, while the mid-20th-century rectory is on the south. I have (and have used) his massive *Commentary on the Book of Ezekiel*. Like me he left Suffolk for inner-London, but for different reasons; he was a member of the Westminster Assembly (1643-52). In what is the same benefice of seven villages, the author, artist and social historian Richard Cobbold (1797-1877) was Rector of Wortham for over 50 years, and the Puritan Bible-commentator Elnathan Parr (1577–?1632) who wrote on the *Epistle to the Romans* as well as *The Grounds of Divinity*, etc, was incumbent of Palgrave.

While not writing in exactly the same rooms, I have had the privilege of praying, preaching and singing more precisely where (in chronological order) my elder brothers Parr, Greenhill, Ridley, Hoole, Cobbold and Charlesworth did so before me; see Hebrews 12:1-2!

INDEX OF SCRIPTURES—main references only:

Trees along the River

9:9–13	61	19:1–10	61	16:11–15	15
11:16–19	69	19:10	51	16:25	12, 32
16:1	68	23–24	76	18:1–3	15
24:27–30	110	24:1–7	71	27	36
28:1–7	71	24:1–35	59		
28:20	13	24:32	49		

Philippians
1:3–6 91
3:7–14 91

Colossians
3:1–4 34
3:16 30, 33

Mark
Whole book 57
1:14–15 58
1:14–18 59, 117
1:16–17 102
2:1–12 61
4:1–2 60
4:35–41 61
6:3 15
8:31–38 70
14–15 74
14:12–26 31
15–16 76
15:24 32
15:33–34 18

John
1:14 63, 64
1:25–26 67
1:29 72
3:3–15 72
3:14–16 70
7:38–39 78
8:31–36 61
12:32–33 53
14:26 73, 78
14:27 77
15:26 73
19–20 75, 76
20 74
20:1 71
20:24–29 48
21 117
21:1–14 58
21:15–17 102

Romans
1:16 85
3:23 25
8:15–23 86
8:18–21 7
8:18–25 3, 9
8:20–23 105
11:33–36 14
12:9–16 87
13:1–7 93

1 Corinthians
3:10–13 28
9:24–27 97
13 88
15:58 28

2 Corinthians
4:1 28
8:9 89

Galatians
4:4–7 87
6:2 88

Ephesians
1:4–14 86
2:4–7 89
2:8 90
5:19–21 30, 33
5:25–27 22

1 Timothy
2:1–3 93

2 Timothy
1:2 94
1:5 41
3:15–16 95
4:11 48, 57

Hebrews
2:12 32
10:24–28 96
11:24–25 16
12:1–2 97

James
Whole letter 98
3:18 99
4:14 35

1 Peter
2:13–17 93
2:24 4
4:10–11 100
4:12–17 101
5:10 103
5:13 57

Luke
1:26–38 62
2 65, 74
2:1–7 63, 64
2:1–16 31
2:1–20 17, 66
2:8–14 110
2:10–11 52
2:25–35 12
2:29 67
2:41–50 68
4:14–19 50
7:11–17 60
8:4–15 39
6:57–62 70

Acts
2 117
2:1–4 78
2:22–25 14, 31
2:41–42 79
4 117
7:51–60 80, 81
8:26–40 82
10:33–43 82, 83
13:5,13 57
15:11 90

INDEX OF SELECTED THEMES:

sight (divine) 19, 24, 29, 86

sight/s (human) 6, 27, 50, 62, 63, 76, 96, 109, 110

sign/s 7, 11, 22, 31, 45, 52, 81, 117

signal 97

Silas 12

silence/t/ly 31, 32, 34, 50, 76, 87, 88

Simeon 12

sin/s 3, 7, 11, 25, 40, 58, 62, 63, 67, 72, 83, 88, 89, 94, 95, 107, 114

Sinai 20

sing/ing *passim*

slave/ry, enslave 3, 14, 47, 54, 55, 61, 62, 93

slow/ness 24, 25, 48, 59, 60, 88, 104

smiles 89

soil (noun) 5, 27, 105

soldiers 4

Son of Man 57, 70, 80, 116

song/s 9, 12, 16, 17, 22, 30–33, 43, 46, 47, 52, 66, 80, 90, 91, 95, 99–101, 111–113

sorrow 19, 39, 43

sovereign/ty 35, 47, 62, 69, 72

space 21, 62, 94, 115

speak/ing (God subject) 19, 20, 31, 56, 65, 70, 73, 78, 82–84, 95, 96, 111, 112

speak (humans subject) 45, 69, 88, 90, 95

speech 20, 72

spice 75

splendour 3

sport 97

spring (season) 3

stain 11, 26, 86

star/s 1, 2, 11, 31, 52, 109

step 34, 75, 91, 102

Stephen 80, 81

Stepney Greencoat 113

steward/s 97, 105

stiles 115

still waters 59

stilling the storm 50, 61

stone 105

storm 26, 36, 50, 91, 105

story, stories 14, 43, 45, 54, 59, 74, 87, 95, 99, 110, 115

stripes 82

stranger/s 17, 54, 108

stream/s 8, 12, 39, 46, 73, 78, 105, 115

Streatham 114

street/s 52, 59, 114

strength/ened 27, 29, 34, 43, 44, 47, 91, 97

struggle/d/s 37, 44, 55, 86, 94

suffer/ed/ing 8, 43, 46, 54, 68, 82, 86, 90, 92, 95, 100, 104, 114

sun 11, 55, 72, 111, 115

sun and moon 31

sun, moon, stars 1, 2

Sun of righteousness 66

Sunday 71

sunlight, sunlit 11, 19

sunrise/sunset 60, 85

sunshine 8, 105

supper 79

surprise/s 6, 41, 65, 103, 105

sustain/ing 15, 22, 27, 28, 37, 55, 105

swift 82, 83, 104

sword 4, 18

sycamore 4

synagogue 60

tabernacle 15

table 4, 59, 117

talent/s 15, 31

talk/ing 21, 41, 42, 50, 84, 107, 108

task 94, 102, 106

teach/ers/ing 33, 34, 41, 42, 51, 53, 59, 60, 68, 70, 82, 94, 100, 104, 107, 113, 115

Teacher (Christ) 51, 60, 74, 111, 112

tears 34, 89, 91, 113, 116

tempest 36

temple 60, 117

tent 72

tent-making 15

tested, testing 94, 97

thanks/giving 7, 15, 27, 30, 35, 39, 41, 42, 54, 62, 67, 71, 81, 92, 108, 113, 114, 116

theory 103

thirsty 8, 47

Thomas 48

thousands 53, 76, 98

thunder 20

tide 36

work/s, divine 1, 2, 15, 22, 27, 28, 36, 38, 47, 51, 62, 65, 70, 82, 103, 106, 107

work/ers, human 1 0 , 15, 24, 27–29, 41, 82, 87, 100, 102, 113, 114, 117

worship(specific) 18, 47, 92, 116

wounds/ed 5, 10, 32, 45, 82, 96

wrath of God 20, 104

wreck/ers/ing 3, 10, 105

write/ing, written 14, 20, 45, 72, 100

year/s 22, 30, 35, 48, 54, 55, 58, 59, 65, 87, 89, 91, 113–116

yesterday 33, 81, 112

Zacchaeus 116

Zion 26, 112

INDEX OF TUNES

INDEX OF CONTEMPORARY COMPOSERS

The name of the LORD revealed from above — T 104

The powers of kings, their robes and rings — W 66

The prophet speaks, the locusts come — W 36

The realm of our much-travelled Lord — T 76

The sacraments Jesus has given us to share — T 79

The saints in Christ are one in every place — L 153

The seasons, Lord, are in your hand — T 21

The Spirit led by day — L 120

The story of Joseph, the favourite son — T 14

The story's never quite complete — T 59

The sun went down on Jacob's grief — L 11

The truth which lives in us by grace — T 107

The victory of our God is won — L 197

The vision of the living God — L 54

The wise man built... When Jesus finished — T 56

The wonder of salvation — L 144

The Word was very God — L 99

The works of the Lord are created in wisdom — L 33

Then I saw a new heaven and earth — L 198

They came to hear the word of God — W 96

They write what many read — T 45

This earth belongs to God — L 211

This is the man who runs with God — W 88

This world has great rewards to give — L 158

Those who rely on the Lord are unshakeable — L 263

Through all the world let Christ be known — L 115

To Christ who once this supper made — L 133

To everyone whom God has made — L 123

To God our strength come, sing aloud — L 230

To know God's mind and do his will — L 112

To set their hearts on God — L 256

To show the world that God is real — T 106

To this we have been called — L 181

To those for whom you lived and died — T 89

To walk the way of Abraham — L 7

Towering over road and river — L 266

Trees along the river — T 8

True light, blazing in the darkest place — L 186

Twelve for the twelve apostles — L 67

Two hundred years have passed — W 84

Two thousand years of sorrow — W 41

Up from the depths I cry to God — L 258

Very early, Sunday morning — T 71

Wake, O wake, and sleep no longer — L 69

Waters, oceans and seas — T 36

We are one in Christ, and can never be at war — W 71

We call him Christ, the Firstborn Son — T 80

We have done wrong, and only God can save us — L 93

We have not walked these paths before — W 78

We heard Christ's word, and looking back — L 132

LOST COIN; LAST WORDS
(One for my publisher)

She lost a coin, one silver coin:
a story grew around it;
she lit her lamp, and swept the house,
and searched until she found it.

Just one in ten, that silver piece,
but every one was precious:
she could not rest till it was safe;
her story comes from Jesus.

Then full of joy, she calls her friends
and quickly tells her neighbours:
'The coin I lost has now been found –
the prize of all my labours!'

Lord, I was lost, I could not move;
your light had reached me never:
you searched my darkness, rescued me
and gave me life for ever.

In earth and heaven, what joy there is
among each shining angel,
when even one who has been lost
is found by God's evangel!

Lord Jesus, yours the costly search
and yours the finished story;
our joy to hear, repent, believe:
to God be all the glory!

8787 iambic: tune: THE FOLLOWERS

Written 22nd Feb 2017: The woman in Luke 15:8–10 is sometimes overlooked in favour of the shepherd and the father. Let her not be overlooked on this final page, nor what the great Storyteller went on to do!

How should I praise thee, Lord? how should my rhymes
  Gladly engrave thy love in steel,
If what my soul doth feel sometimes,
  My soul might ever feel!

George Herbert

I will sing to the LORD, for he has been good to me.

Psalm 12:6